Healing With Energy

Healing With Energy

The Definitive Guide to Hands-On Techniques From a Master

Starr Fuentes

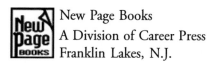

New Page Books
A Division of Career Press
Franklin Lakes, N.J.

HEALING WITH ENERGY
EDITED AND TYPESET BY GINA TALUCCI
Cover design by Lucia Rossman/Digi Dog Design NYC
Printed in the U.S.A. by Book-mart Press

To order this title, please call toll-free 1-800-CAREER-1 (NJ and Canada: 201-848-0310) to order using VISA or MasterCard, or for further information on books from Career Press.

The Career Press, Inc., 3 Tice Road, PO Box 687,
Franklin Lakes, NJ 07417
www.careerpress.com
www.newpagebooks.com

Library of Congress Cataloging-in-Publication Data

Fuentes, Starr.
    Healing with energy : the definitive guide to hands-on techniques
from a master / by Starr Fuentes
        p. cm.
    Includes index.
    ISBN-13: 978-1-56414-969-5
    ISBN-10: 1-56414-969-2
        1. Energy medicine. I. Title.

RZ421.F84 2007
615.8'2—dc22

                                                    2007016601

To Esperanza, who is still alive in my heart, and will forever be through her teachings.

Acknowledgments

I gratefully acknowledge my husband, Art Jackson, for his love and support, as well as all of my other teachers.

Thank you to the following people for the many hours of love, dedication, and service: Selena Rodriguez, Kirke vom Scheidt, Gabriele Bodmer, Inge Pfeifer, Brooke Still, Nancy Burson, Bianca Guerra, Mary Lyn Hammer, Zabe Barnes, James Robinson, Zoe Cochran, Pat Childers, Jodi Sorota, Shirley Resler, Collette Chase, Eileen Miller, and all my students and clients.

Also, thank you to Ja-lene Clark, and also to the staff at New Page Books, especially Laurie Kelly-Pye and Michael Pye, for their support in the publication of this work.

Contents

Part Two: The Healer's Toolbox

The Healer's Creed

I believe that Source uses me as a vessel and a conduit, providing light, healing, and love to the healee.

I believe that Source has a bigger picture and knows the highest good for all concerned; I am serving as an instrument for Source.

I believe that knowing the core issue or original cause of the disease and owning it may let the energy of the disease go gently, quickly, and easily.

I know that the four elements have to be whole for healing to progress.

Air, represented by the quality of air we breathe, by the choice of the words from our lips, by thoughts sent out to gather more like thoughts.

Earth, represented by our personal environment, the food that we eat, the possessions that surround us, the type of clothes that we wear.

Water, by the quality of water that we drink, how we bathe, and the flow of our tears.

Fire, represented by how we pursue our purpose, the passion and compassion we have for others, commitments and discipleship for our path.

The words that come from our mouths may be sharp, soft, loving, or hard. I know that intention and follow-through lay a deep foundation for healing. As a healer I must be the conduit, which is my work, and refrain from thinking that I have any control over the healing.

And most importantly,

I will give solutions, not answers,

so without me the healee knows how to BE HEALING.

Introduction

ealing is a mysterious process. For some people it comes instantly, while for others it never happens. Healing can come in the simplest forms, such as a smile; touch; or timely, kind, and appropriate words. You can even heal another by listening to them completely in the now. Healing can also come through a vibration, technique, or herbal or homeopathic remedy. Ultimately though, the real healing occurs only between the person being healed (healee) and Source.

It can be challenging at times to bring the healing energies from Source to you, because, as the healee, you may lack the chemistry or the capability for connecting with Source in a certain way. In these situations you need a healer—someone or something to run that missing energy from Source to you. Healers serve as a conduit between the healing energies of Source and the healee.

Healing With Energy is derived from my five decades of work as a master healer, and from teaching more than 10,000 students about being a healer. In this manual, healers will learn about a healing session from beginning to end along with information about the energies at work in a healing, and hand positions that facilitate healing. The intermediate healer will find that this book serves as a quick reference to the ways Source works with techniques to promote healing. I have personally used all of the techniques you will learn about. These techniques are gathered from all over the world, mostly from my teachers; some are from my students who shared their knowledge with me.

Throughout the world, I have found that there are many, many ways to heal, and no single practice is better than the rest. Some of the techniques work more specifically in precise areas and with particular types of people or diseases, while others work with mental, emotional, and spiritual planes, which have to change first, before the physical body does.

You will read about absolute rules, such as the role of intention in healing. The term *intention overrides technique* is the agreement that exists between the subconscious and unconscious mind of the healer to connect with Source and Earth in order to facilitate a healing. Also, note that if you forget a step or reverse steps during whatever technique you employ, the subconscious and unconscious mind will automatically adjust the energy for the highest good of the healer and the healee.

As you study the techniques and become more practiced as a healer, you will find that you do some of the processes automatically, such as connecting to Source and Earth and cleansing yourself before a healing. Eventually, as you gather experiences and perfect your intentions as a healer, people start to heal the moment they walk into the room.

—Starr Fuentes
2008

Part One:

The Healing Session

Chapter One

The Role of the Healer

What is healing? Healing can come in many forms, and you will learn so much about being a healer in this manual—from the things you need to remember; to building your awareness of the energies, fields, and processes of healing; and finally to the techniques and exercises you can master as you further develop your skills as a healer.

When you look at energy and at the mechanics of quantum physics, you can begin to understand several important things about healing. In quantum physics a particle turns into a wave, and that wave turns into a particle. When you make something matter to you mentally, emotionally, physically, and spiritually, it becomes matter. If it is important to you what the neighbors think, then the neighbors will think something about you. It matters to you; it manifests on Earth, and often inside the body.

When you let go of an energy by forgiving, or acknowledging that "matter" exists, then the matter can be turned into another energy, and the energy can be turned into any direction that you choose in your life. When you guilt and shame other people, and choose not to be responsible for your reality, then the matter is put into other people's hands and there is no way that you can heal or change it back into a vitalized energy. When you become responsible for your own energy and what matters to you, then you have the capacity to change it.

What are you most suited to heal?

Some people possess natural athletic abilities, while others are more naturally suited to be healers. If I had an interest in becoming an athlete at an early age, my life path would have been motivated by very different energies. The life experiences I attracted would have been nothing like those that I have lived as a teacher, healer, and student.

The personal experiences you have gathered on the life path that you have taken up until now will also determine the type of healer you are naturally suited to be. Whether athlete or healer, the more you exercise and expand your innate abilities, the more enhanced your performance will become.

To be healed is the choice of the healee. The healer is the connection between the healee and Source. A conduit—that's what the word *healer* means—energy, a conduit of light.

Some of the greatest healers can heal others with their presence alone. Others may use their voice, touch, teachings, art, books, thoughts, hands, music, or prayers to heal. Healing can be so many things, even simple, well-timed words moving from Source through you. As a healer, you are most suited to heal others of the things that you have personally healed from or with experiences that have touched your life significantly. You will draw healees who need to be healed in the areas of which you have completed your own healings, and you will go through periods when you will magnetize the same disease or symptoms over and over again with healee after healee.

Becoming a conduit

The primary or main function of a healer is to be a conduit for Source and Earth energies. The healer becomes an integral part of the fields that raise and complete the vibrations to facilitate the healing processes. You are like a television set. You, as a healer, are not the big picture. You are not the viewer. The quality of your individual healing equipment is composed of your personal standards. The resolution depends on how many solutions you have found to your *own* challenges. The amount of channels that you are capable of receiving depends on your ability to open up, expand, switch, and seek new channels. Your lack of judgments and limitations will create color, and the size of your screen is proportionate to your clear intention to heal. The more you personally heal yourself, the more access you have to other channels, and therefore it will become easier to sense what is going on with the healee.

As a piece of living equipment, it is up to you to maintain your quality and operational ability. Fine-tuning begins each time you work with a new healee. With time, connecting with Spirit to heal will be as easy as turning on the television. The specific channel to tune into for the healing will be given to you by Spirit with each healing.

> The word healer is simply a word.
>
> Keep your ego out of the way.

Chapter Two

What Healers Need to Know About Healees

he healee is the person to whom you are directing the energy from Source. The first and most critically important point to discuss about our human healees is that free will is to be respected. Each being is exactly where they are supposed to be at this moment in time. If you drop your judgments and view them from a soul level, you may understand the Divine plan no matter how "bad" the situation may seem. When you understand that the soul is experiencing an intentional developmental lesson, you honor their free will; for example, some people's soul contracts include teaching compassion through their example of how NOT to be as they die. Keep your judgments out of the way; no matter what it looks, feels, or sounds like, the healing will or will not happen on the physical plane according to the terms of the soul contract.

Healing friends, family, and loved ones

You may get some great results using the techniques in *Healing With Energy* on family members, close friends, or your spouse. For optimal healing in general, it is advisable to ask someone outside your friend/family circle to work on them. This is because family members share the same or similar genetic and energetic patterns. When the healer and the healee share these patterns in a healing session, it is more difficult for the healer to bring through the appropriate energies to achieve results. In other words, these very similar patterns may get in the way of the healing energies.

In relationships with our close friends and spouses, there comes a point of depth where we consciously or subconsciously develop certain biases, and also shared DNA. The bias could be that we love this person so much that we desperately want to see the healing happen, even if this is not in alignment with the greatest good for all concerned. The healee might not be conscious of the outcome they most need, and your fears of losing this person or seeing them experience pain may get in the way. The bottom line on healing family, friends, and loved ones is that DNA, feelings, or thoughts about this person can detract from the healer doing his or her job, which is being a clear conduit of healing Source energy. The best way to heal your own genetic and energetic patterns is to heal yourself and then model your own healing for friends, family, and loved ones to follow.

Getting permission

The healer should not force healings on people. Before a healing, the healee must first ask clearly for the healing. Sometimes the healee will come to you for advice, and then come back again and again for more advice on the same situation, yet they will not have put that advice into action. This is a form of asking for a healing. It is important to understand that when people complain about something, they are not asking for a healing. They must ask you how to change it before you can work on them.

Types of healees

Healees will respond to the energy coming from Source through you in various ways.

You may encounter many combinations or hybrids of the various types of healees covered in this chapter. These simple suggestions are appropriate no matter what type you encounter:

☆ Keep the healee focused on breath.

☆ Let go and let Source control the healing.

☆ Keep your focus on the energy flow, not the healee.

Hard worker

These healees work so hard, and they have so much of their own energy flowing, that there is virtually no room for the energy from Source. It is important to get these healees to relax and focus on their breathing. They will use motion of the body to channel the energy of Source rather than letting the energy flow naturally into the places it needs to be. Do not confuse this with the healee who works with the energy to let it flow into the places that the energy wants to go. The healee who is working with the energy will not repeat a movement over and over again.

Cold/white

These healees will turn extremely white and hold all the energy inside. The effect is that they feel "colder" as the healing progresses. These types of people have a tremendous fear of change, and will breathe in shallow breaths. Their bodies will be rigid and they will probably not move. If you rock the body gently at different points of the healing, the energy they are holding on to may gradually loosen, and the energy from Source will slowly and surely move into the healee. Get this healee to breathe deeply and stay focused on their breath. You will probably need to remind them several times to breathe.

Chatty

These healees want to talk throughout the healing. Consciously or unconsciously they want to control the healing, and they want you to do it their way. They will give you all sorts of fantastic reasons for moving your hands and shifting the way you're directing the energy. Gently remind them that Source is in charge of the healing, and their job is to focus on their breath. Usually these people are healers or teachers themselves.

Cough/spit

These healees cannot seem to connect the head and the body. They move used energy out through their throat by coughing or spitting it out of their mouths. This type usually gets "chunks" of healing. Encourage them to spit and cough as much as possible, and know it will usually take multiple sessions to complete a full healing. After several sessions, they will stop coughing and spitting, and when they do, remind them to focus their energy in the heart so that you will prepare them for the major chunk of healing energy that they will receive to fill in the spot.

Rebel/resister

These healees will probably go through all the motions of healing while they dispose the energy elsewhere, so they can hang on to it. Sometimes these healees focus on their breath so much that it is exaggerated. You will sense no movement of energy, and when you express that, they will respond with, "I'm doing my best" or "I don't know how." Sometimes abandonment works with this type. Tell the healee that you are working harder than they are, then quit and walk away. These healees fear the unknown, and will usually make changes if they have a detailed description of the healing processes and the results that they may expect. Watch these people and you will learn much from them—they are masters of manipulation, and can create distraction at the drop of a pan. The rebel/resister has perfected the avoidance of every Earth and Source energy.

Crier/screamer

These healees have been trained to move energy around by using their emotions. These behaviors should not be encouraged, discouraged, or acknowledged. *During a healing, under no circumstances should you rub or pat anyone who is crying*, because this can plug people into their sexual abuse issues. Patting or physically consoling is detrimental to the healing process because focusing on these issues eats up the healing energy from Source that could be directed elsewhere, and this will not help raise the vitality of the healee's body.

Traveler

These healees leave their bodies the moment the healing starts. Travelers are challenging due to the difficulty of getting a sense of how the healing is going because you can't easily tell where they are. You may have to work hard to intuit what is really going on with this energy. Because the travelers are not in their bodies, it's harder for a healer to determine where the energy should go. Caution: these types of healees leave their bodies in a shield that says they are in good shape; you need to get past that shield.

Swallower

These healees let the energy move the blocks within their systems up, leading to the way out. When the energy reaches the throat, they swallow their pattern because subconsciously they want to keep this energy. Remind them not to swallow, and explain that they are swallowing and retaining an old pattern.

Clencher

These healees will allow the energies to move out of their bodies. When you check, it is gone. They have a secret though: They keep the energy that should be disposed of within their closed fists, and put it back after the healing is over. In their hands, they hide the negative energy, pain, or core issues energy, so it is not instantly apparent for a healer to sense it in their bodies. Also, watch for women and long-haired men who, at the end of a healing, put the energy in their hair. They usually do this by twisting locks or moving their hair in an intense movement.

Scruncher

These healees will let all the used energy move up their face, and will contort the muscles in the face to hold the energy. It will look as though all the features of the face are in one 4-inch circle. Gently smooth down the muscles in the face while running the energy with your other hand. This healee will find it difficult to cry although their eyes may fill with water. Encourage them to cry (do not pat them), and wait until several tears have rolled down the face. The scruncher may even deny that they are crying with nonsense statements: "My eyes are leaking" or "I have something in my eye." If the healee makes statements of denial, remain silent and keep the energy flowing.

Assumptions

No matter what type of healees you are working with, do not assume that they are broken. Use your knowledge about, and experience with, energy to see, feel, or hear what is going on so that you will be informed with the facts that they might not even be consciously aware of. People will frequently tell you that they are dis-eased when this is not actually true. Often the source of the dis-ease is an ingrained and outdated belief system of theirs that needs to be eliminated.

Do not assume that your healee is healthy. People who appear to be healthy can also exhibit an aura of nonvitality. Although his or her life seems to be in order, it may not be so true. Check it out.

Four questions

Before the session, ask your healee these four questions and have them write down the answers. The purpose is so they can begin a conversation with the matter they want to heal:

☆ What is your challenge?

☆ How do you know you have it?

☆ What have you done about it?

☆ What are you going to do about it next?

It is important that you do not use these exact words every time with every healee, and that you paraphrase the questions and let the answers come out of the mouth of the healee.

Final note

The healee will get more from a session when he or she has a material investment in the healing, so it is important that you charge for healing sessions. You will find that those you work on for free will not take the healing as seriously as the people who have an energetic or financial investment in the healing.

> As a healer, you are simply the conduit for healing energies. Source and the healee are doing the real work.

Chapter Three
Connecting to the Four Energies

Establishing a clean and clear connection to the four energies or forces is required if you are to realize the strongest possible healings. During the healing process, agreements are made with these energies that may or may not be spoken of or consciously received by the healer or the healee. The combined power of these four energies creates the forces that will work together to provide the most complete healing possible. If any one of these energies is out of alignment with the full power of light, or not working in unison, then the quality of the healing will be severely diminished or nullified.

Four healing energies and forces

Source—ask and you shall receive

There are many ways to ask Source to receive energy. At times, a sincere intention to heal is enough of a signal to Source. At other times, asking from your heart and with the deepest gratitude for life creates a profound connection with Source. Most importantly, walk your talk and you will become a conduit for the healing energies of life. You know you are connected to Source when your life flows smoothly (no bumping into things, tripping over things, and so on).

Yourself—intention of the healer overrides technique

An agreement exists with your higher and lower self that allows you to serve as the conduit for the energies from Source. There is also an agreement with your ego to stay out of the way while you are serving as the conduit for Source. The agreement, which exists with your higher and lower self, was initiated during your soul contract, and it is the one that tends to vacillate the most.

Healee—grants permission to be healed

The agreement from the healee requires that he or she will allow you to work on him or her, and that he or she is willing to be at ease throughout the process.

Earth—access through conscious connection

We are connected to Earth because we have a body. The Earth is one of the most powerful tools available to the well-grounded healer. Earth takes the used energies that are emitted during a healing and recycles them into new energies that are appropriate to be used elsewhere. Earth decides the highest good for the reuse of these energies. The importance of staying grounded during a healing is critical and cannot be overstated. Healers will receive the new energies from Earth that are necessary to facilitate changes on the physical plane. As you receive the energies from Source above through your crown chakra, you can facilitate the change of thoughts and emotions that originally created the dis-ease and the belief systems that maintain the dis-ease.

Becoming aware of your connection

There are a few rules to discuss that will raise the quality and the quantity of the healing energies that come through you. Reach outward and inward simultaneously for these energies, for they exist in the Universe as well as reside within you. When you connect to these forces, it is important to know that they are in abundance everywhere, and there is plenty for everyone. The moment that you have a judgment about any aspect that is part of the healing, you will separate from Source energies. As a healer, each judgment gets in the way of healing and limits the quality of the energies coming from Source through you.

The awareness of how these forces move through you and the conscious connection that you create before each healing will last until the moment you move out of NOW time. Make a commitment to be fully aware of the moment that your thoughts go into the future or the past, or if a judgment surfaces. If that happens, stop and reestablish your connection to the four forces.

Exercise to reconnect

Stand up in the middle of the room and take notice of everything around you. Notice that the floor is supporting your body. Notice the windows letting light in. Notice the ceiling and the walls.

Then notice everything else in the room. How does the furniture make your life easier? What is in the room to add beauty? What objects are there for function? Continue to take note of everything else.

To cocreate a physical plane healing, you must be supported by a floor or foundation where the energy from Earth can enter your body. Notice the air above your head and the ceiling. There is an invisible connection to Source that keeps us standing up through feeding the body energies. This energy is also necessary for healing. Now close your eyes; in your mind make a list of everything in the room. Now open your eyes and inventory what you have forgotten. Even though you forgot to list these objects, they still remain in the room.

In healing, objects surrounding us are similar to intention: They exist to provide function and comfort for us. Whether we acknowledge their existence or not, they are energies that are actively present at all times. Notice that your very presence as a healer gives you permission to ask and receive the energies necessary for healing. Know that your intention to heal will override the technique you employ.

Forever present

Once you have learned a technique, it is forever present. It will be there even if you do not remember it consciously. You are usually given enough permission to do the healing when the healee asks you for a session. Before you start your healing, notice that if you think about Source and Earth for a moment, you will know that they are present with you all the time; be aware that you (the ego) is all that can get in the way.

The only things that will limit your healing power are you and your ability to maintain a NOW connection with the four energies.

Chapter Four

Negotiating the Fields of Healing

A force is an energy that moves along with a current, while a field is a container for energy. The fields in a healing session are formed from the combined energies of all forces and all people present in the healing situation. The field of integrity is the most important aspect during the healing. As you will learn, when your integrity is incomplete, there are many ways that you use, leak, and consume energy before it reaches the healee.

Several fields exist and are present in a healing session. In this chapter, we will look at what composes the basic fields in which most healings occur, along with the chakra system and the aura.

Basic fields of healing

One of the most neglected pieces of information about healing are the three basic fields that are created by the healer, healee, and the forces.

Space

This is the physical space or area in which the healing is happening. It includes the energies that are present from the building, the building's owner, and past events that have occurred in this space. The quality of the air, smells, and sounds will affect the space you are using to create the healing field.

Resonance

As all the energies in a healing session combine, they form the field of resonance. This field is resonate to a vibratory rate of the healer and the healee, which is a combination of all the forces that are at play along with the innate energies that apply to that specific healing. The overall quality of the healing depends on your awareness of the energies present, and your ability to use them for the highest good of all concerned.

Outcome

Trust that the outcome of the healing will be exactly what it is supposed to be. In certain healings, physical transmutation occurs; in other healings, energies are shifted in the higher levels to create the structure that is in alignment with the person's soul contract. Sometimes you will not see, feel, or know that a healing has happened. Be assured that it has.

Aura

The aura is a collection of vibrations that are created by our thoughts, actions, and deeds. Understand that if you choose not to act upon something, that in and of itself is an action, therefore it becomes part of your aura. The aura holds the grossest of vibrations, from the beating of the heart, the movement of the blood through the body, the movement of the lungs, to the subtlest of vibrations, a faint knowing that something is inappropriate, a slight sense of discomfort in another person, and an open-ended psychic question.

The awesome luminescence of a spiritual master's aura, and the dirty, dingy aura of a broken, homeless person, are the consequences of the person's ability to respond to life. The auras did not start out as luminous or dingy through a series of choices or nonchoices, of acting or reacting to the challenges of life. Their auras became an expression of the way they have handled life.

Using the analogy of a car, the aura is the engine that gathers our thoughts, intentions, disciplines, resistances, fears, and rebellions; it starts magnetizing or moving us toward situations in life where these energies can be expressed in the material plane. Your aura is like the inside of your car. It can show the trash of what you have not let go of, the dirt of negligence, and the energy of organization or impeccability. It speaks loudly of how you manifest your life. In the aura, be it appropriate or inappropriate, there are energies that have not been dealt with.

If you choose to learn about the colors, different thought forms, and significant marks, lesions, and holes in the aura, make sure that you use two to three different sources. What is potent and important for you to keep in mind is that the state of the aura is the future state of the body. The two places where disease appears one year before it materializes in the body are the irises of the eyes and the aura.

Chakra system

The word *chakra* comes from the Sanskrit word meaning "wheel." A chakra is a receptor and a vortex that receives, perceives, and filters energies from you and the world around you. When you subconsciously or consciously choose to deal, or not to deal, with energies, you choose whether your chakras will be healthy, vital, malfunctioning, or shut down.

There are many books written about the chakras; read a few. You can find charts on the internet that tell you specific details about each chakra. I am going to tell you what they don't tell you. Know that the following paragraphs are in addition to anything else you have already learned about chakras. It would be a good idea for you to be very familiar with chakras before you read the rest of this section, and, if you are not, skip these next few paragraphs.

Research and development department

The chakras are the research and development department for making excellent decisions and choices in your life. Their capacity to pick up fine, subtle, and hidden vibrations is awe-inspiring. The multitude of facts, statements, and data that the chakras send every moment to the subconscious and unconscious mind is staggering. When we make decisions, we think that we know why (consciously). The real reason we make decisions is from the subconscious/unconscious input that the chakras deliver through the subconscious and unconscious mind.

In our modern-day quest for instant gratification and making things easy and comfortable, we throw monkey wrenches into the chakra system. After understanding that denial, apathy, and avoidance injected into a chakra is like sticking a finger into an electric socket, our chakras would be in a healthy, vital condition.

The general lack of information about chakras and health sends more people to therapy than do parental issues. As a healer, a keen sense of the healee's chakra system is essential to the overall support of the healing.

Centering within the fields

The healing session is an opportunity for the healee to be at ease, and it is the healer's responsibility to create the space for healing. The challenge for the healer is to remain aware of the tension in the field, and stay centered. As the healee begins to respond to the forces that are in play, and the wave of healing is in full progress, change occurs. When the dis-ease moves out of the healee's body, it moves into the field and then out through the earth. At times, depending on the integrity level of the field, the energy will leave the healee faster than the field can dissipate by asking that the healing move gently, easily, and quickly.

Experiencing the fields

One of the best ways to become an excellent healer is by practicing and working on healing yourself. As an experienced healer, your ease with the dis-ease of the healee is a critical piece. First-hand experiences with healing yourself will help you become more at ease with all the forces and energies present during a healing. This is why a healer is most suited to heal others of which they have healed themselves, for the more you heal yourself, the more energy you can conduct through you from Source. As the blending of the energies and forces occur, the healing takes place. This blending results in a higher sense of ease in the healee, which occurs at a much greater level than before the healing. On some level, the healer should monitor the levels of energies in the field as the healing progresses.

Work first to heal yourself, and the end result will be that you have enough clarity to facilitate the forces in raising the energy level of you both.

> When you heal yourself first, then your ability
> to heal others dramatically increases.

Chapter Five

How the Energies Work

There is abundant discussion about the concept of energy in the spiritual texts. In this chapter, you will explore the vitalizing and devitalizing energies, and look at energy from several different perspectives. This knowledge will help you form a foundation for dealing with the light sources that all of us use at light speed.

We all know the five *heavy* senses of taste, touch, vision, smell, and hearing. Five *light* senses also exist. Usually, a beginning healer will have a natural tendency to display at least one of the five light senses. As healer's mature, the aspiration grows to master all five senses discussed in this chapter.

Five light senses

Charismatic

This is the light sense that is the hardest to explain. The charismatic light sense keeps reminding you that there is more to know and more to do in the situation. This light sense keeps us fascinated with the healing process and interested in even the most boring times. This energy has a profound effect on the healee. The effect of a few words from a charismatic healer will inspire the healee to make a significant change in his or her life. Charismatic energy lets you know that there is an answer to our deepest questions.

Electric

This is the light sense that seems to be giving in every situation. Similar to electricity, the electric light sense carries a charge. Healers that are electric seem to be busy doing and adding energy in all manners of form, or to whomever they are interacting with. The electric light sense is the one that turns peoples' heads to see what has changed the energy in a room when someone enters. By its heightened sense of awareness, this light sense will let you know when to change the direction of your focus in public. This sense is responsible for the hair on your arms standing on end in certain situations. The electric lets you feel the energy moving from healer to healee. Electric healers tend to "zap" people and diseases with their healing energies. Two electric healers may give each other a small shock. If someone touches you and you jump, that is electric energy.

Magnetic

This light sense is the energy that pulls you and your hands almost automatically toward specific spots on the healee. It is the light sense that is activated immediately after a person comes into your presence, and you ask if they are all right. The magnetic energy pulls people into the magnetic healer's arms for a hug. Strangers will start conversations with magnetic healers about their problems. These healers take on the mother and nurturer roles—overdoing these roles can cause the magnetic healer to try to fix the healee, rather than allowing the energy to flow between Source and the healee. Out of the five types of light senses, magnetic healers need to focus specifically and diligently on cleansing, grounding, and connecting. Dealing with strong magnetic energy is a challenge, because magnetic energy can pull us into the "stuff" of the healee. The challenge of the magnetic healer is to heal without taking on the energy of the healee. Be aware that if you become pulled into the healee's stuff, you are no longer serving as healer; you have become a healee.

Electromagnetic

This is the light sense that evaluates the push and pull of the energy in the healee. This energy is extremely powerful because as the needs of the healee shift, so does the ebb and flow of electromagnetic energy. At times, this energy can be steadily balanced, and at others the percentage of electric and magnetic energies will fluctuate depending on what is coming through from Source. A keen awareness of electromagnetic energy allows the healer to accurately access blockage. A healer that uses electromagnetic energy can be valueable in almost all types of healings. Electromagnetic energy has the same energy as the tides of the ocean—and the same care is needed to become aware of when the healer is being pulled into the undertow of the healee's stuff.

Presence

This is the light sense that, when strongly developed, can heal and affect others who are simply present in this being's energy field. The type of energy from Source that comes through presence provides a feeling of all around well-being. These types of healers are the ones who everyone seems to love to converse and be with.

People with presence have so incorporated the presence into their personality that, often, they hardly know that they are healers. They think they simply have a good sense of humor and love to make people feel good. Presence is a wide, soft, feel-good beam. A presence healer can become very comfortable with not using words, however, note that sometimes it is very beneficial for the healee to hear a few words from the healer.

Light sense wavelengths

Energy will take the form of one of the light senses after it comes from Source and enters the body. The light senses enter the healee altered, focused, thinned, thickened, spread, and modulated by the specific technique used by the healer.

The light senses are in all parts of your subtle bodies, and each sense will react with a particular wavelength. The energy or the "wave" will behave similar to ocean waves—there will be crests and troughs to the energy.

The crest part of the wave is when the energy is increasing to the highest amplitude and wattage that the healee can handle. All the body systems and energy systems of the healee are absorbing energy. At this point in time, the healer is still raising the amount of energy that is being channeled from Source.

The trough part of the wave is when the energy from Source seems to diminish. All the healee's body and energy systems— that is, aura and meridians—are integrating the energy. At the moment of the trough, it is important for the healer to let go and let the integration process happen. This is not a time to push the energies, or to open wider to Source.

The trough times are perfect for cleaning the energy of the healing field, because at this time, the used energy is moving out of the healee.

After being in the trough, the healer will once again sense the energies of Source coming through them to the healee; now it is time for techniques. The subtle bodies of the healee are ready to absorb light and energy at a greater level, and the healer can gently, easily, and quickly raise the incoming energies.

Outside energies

Often a noise or a movement in the room shifts the integrity of the healing field. Trust that there are no accidents. In my personal experience, I can't count the number of times that a pet has come into the field to point out an important energy of which I was unaware. The times that I forgot to turn off the phone have served to help shift my awareness to a place on the healee that was not receiving enough energy. I have learned that when I lose the wave of the session, an interruption will occur to guide me to reconnecting with the wave again.

The energy that moves throughout the healing process can be incorporated into a session by making statements such as:

☆ All things happening are a part of this healing.

☆ Each distraction will let us connect to our healing in a greater manner.

☆ As we become one with Source, everything becomes one with us.

☆ Sounds and movement amplify the fine-tuning of Source.

Energy flow

Energy is present everywhere. Energy is flowing in your outer universe and your inner universe, constantly expanding or contracting. There is energy in your movements, voice, and thoughts. The most vital energy you will use in healing is the energy of thought. When your thought is connected to Source, and your intention to heal is strong and clear, healing occurs no matter what technique you are employing.

This is the first rule of healing: intention overrides technique.

This rule says that the one thing you really need to heal yourself or anyone else is your strong connection to Source, so that the healing energies will flow through you. Remember that as the healer, you *serve as* a conduit for the healing energies. Through the healing process, it is critical that you maintain the position of conduit, and stay connected to Source. The bottom line is: healing occurs between Source and the healee.

Staying connected to Source involves five simple practices that you follow during the session:

☆ Stay in the NOW.

☆ Gently maintain focus on the flow of energy.

☆ Use essence words in your thoughts (for example, *truth*, *healing*, and *love*).

☆ Be present and feel the energy flow through you to the healee from Source.

☆ Come from your heart, not your head.

Ride the waves

Energy has a resonate rate of flow, which will differ with each healing. Become aware of this resonate rate, and let the energy take you with it, rather than forcing the energy. There will be points in time where you will know that the healee has taken in all that they can absorb at that level. This is the appropriate time to allow the trough of the wave to complete its cycle. As the trough of the wave comes to completion, this is the time to bring the energies up to a higher level.

If you remember one thing about energy, remember that, similar to sound and light, energy is a wave. You must ride the wave through its crest and troughs, because this is the way the energy reaches inside to heal the healee. Riding the wave means you notice when the amount of energy the healee can absorb is diminishing

Healing With Energy

naturally. At this point, most novice healers attempt to keep the energy at the peak of the wave. However, this is the time of the trough or integration. Allow this to happen.

Your awareness as a healer (the body is in the trough of the energy wave and is integrating this energy to heal), will open up the healee for a quicker healing. By not forcing the energy and letting it build again, you will activate the natural healing processes of the healee's body. Once you elevate the subtle bodies to a rate where you can once again let the energy flow through you at a high rate, you will experience another wave and another wave, and so on.

At times, you will intuit shifts in the energies as the body of the healee opens up to take more energy in its process of healing. With any light sense you employ, remember to let the energy flow *through* you, and do not force more energy into the healee's body. You will shift and continue to feel the changes in the energies as you reposition your energies to align with the resonance of Source.

Awareness of the light senses at work through you will significantly increase your abilities as a powerful conduit of healing energy from Source.

Chapter Six

Using the Elements
for Transformation

here are four basic Elements to work with during the healing process. These Elements are the driving catalysts for the transformation of matter. Each
time there is a change on the physical plane, one of
these Elements is involved directly or in conjunction with the laws of physics. These Four Elements
have long been considered sacred in many traditions, especially in the Far East, for a reason. Con-
sider reading about Ayurvedic healing if your
information on the Elements is minimal.

The Four Elements

Air

Air is the quickest, gentlest, and easiest Element to use. Therefore, many beginning healers first master the use of Air before moving into the other Elements. For healers who are experienced, but may not have used Air, work with it for a while and observe the efficiency and quick results you get by using it.

Air seems to know how to get in through even the smallest opening. Most of the body uses oxygen in one form or another, and Air carries vitality, allowing the body's natural healing functions to activate. Used energy is absorbed by Air, and quickly carried out of the energy system.

When you are working on yourself, Air has very little effect. However, when healee and healer get together, the healer provides the momentum from Source to activate the movement of Air as a filtering system. The lower subtle bodies use Air to then remove the devitalizing energies from the healee.

A time when the power of Air is at its strongest is right before a storm, due to the quantity of electric charge and ozone present. I strongly recommend that as a healer, one of the best things you can do is get outside before a storm. You will experience the difference in your subtle bodies almost immediately. This exercise builds recognition that may help you to identify the Air energy at work when healing someone.

This Element can be a gentle breeze smoothing out rough edges, or a raging tornado that can tear a tumor to shreds. To practice making Air your friend, call upon this Element to aid you, so that your healings can be gentle, easy, and quick.

The main side effects from a healer who is using Air to conduct energy from Source is that you will burp, yawn, sneeze, or flatulate.

Healing With Energy

You will also notice that the healee's stomach will growl as the Air moves through the organs in the abdomen.

Later, in the Healer's Toolbox section, we will discuss using Air in combination with the other Elements, and the different colors to fine-tune the energies to the greatest degree for healing.

Water

Water is a flowing Element. Water tends to fill and cleanse any area it can access, and it can carry most of the light energy through its ability to conduct energy. The "wave" is carried by Water, and can aid people who need to recognize where and how the energy is flowing during the healing session. Water flushes and floods areas in which devitalized energies have collected throughout a short or long period of time. Small quantities of Water energy are easier for the healer to control and use in a vitalizing manner. When a healer uses the Water Element, both the healee and the healer's noses may run. They may urinate often, cry, and even throw up. This will happen because the toxins and used energies move away from the healee to the nearest body of water.

Water is not to be used with ulcers, bleeding, and any disease that takes the form of excess liquids, because it will further aggravate the condition.

Fire

Fire is one of the quicker Elements. Using Fire is challenging in that, once you get the energy flowing, it may be hard to get it extinguished. Fire has a tendency to consume everything in its path. Sometimes Fire cannot discern between vital and devitalizing energies, so it will consume both. Fire takes a tremendous amount of energy to maintain. Sometimes healers think that the heat they and the healee feel is from the healer's hand. The heat is from the devitalizing and used energies that are being moved out of the healee by Source.

When Fire is being used, there is a tendency for both the healer and the healee to get hot. The temperature in the room may even increase by as little as one degree, and as much as five degrees. Fire consumes large quantities of energy, and is not gentle on a healer.

Do not use the Element of Fire to heal babies or any dis-ease where heat is present. There is a valid reason for the cliché "you can't fight fire with fire." Fighting Fire with Fire can lead to an overload of the healee's system, and damage to the body of the healee.

When you are working with a healee who lacks motivation or inspiration, fire will ignite the healee's forward motion. Fire burns away devitalized energies and brings new vitality into the healee's life.

Earth

Earth is the most stable and grounded Element. Earth is basically composed of the energy of presence that was introduced earlier, although all five of the light senses are present in the different minerals of the earth. When the Earth Element is in certain shapes, it is formidable like mountains are to earth, and cancer is to the body. Certain energies can cause Earth to lose form. Yet, because Earth can crack and blow away, it is important for the healer to be aware as to whether the healee is absorbing Earth or not. If you are working with someone who is a "spiritual drama queen," these people are often up in the air. Helping them to balance by utilizing Earth energies can result in an extremely powerful healing for them. It helps anchor their spirit to Earth.

When a healer uses earth Energy consciously or unconsciously, the healer takes the dis-ease into him- or herself. Sometimes when the healer is of a very high vitality level, they can transform a nonchronic dis-ease in a few days. If you are not an experienced healer, working with the Earth Element can have ramifications that last for days after the healing. Earth moves the slowest, so the session for the healer will last beyond the session, as it will take more time and energy for the healee's devitalized energies to move through the healer. A clear, practiced healer can work effectively with Earth when they are clear and present enough to understand the universal laws by which energy abides.

Understanding Elemental power

You can use your understanding of the powers of the Four Elements to your advantage. Know that when the healee has a physical manifestation of dis-ease, healing will be a gentler process when the healer, rather than the healee, creates or calls in the Element to facilitate the transformation of the dis-ease to ease. As a healer, it is useful to identify which Element or Elements you most naturally and easily work with. Many healers work primarily with one Element, though this is not a hard and fast rule. Most healers can expand their repertoire to work with all of the Elements, and some healers choose to specialize. If you choose to specialize in a particular Element, be especially conscious of who your healees are and what Element they need in order to heal. For example, if an alcoholic healee goes to a water healer, it is essential that the water healer either use a different Element other than Water, or tell the healee that he or she is not the optimal healer for him or her, and refer the healee to another healer.

When a change on the physical plane occurs, one of the Four Elements is involved.

Chapter Seven

Move Energies by Grounding

Grounding is the process of staying in touch with the physical, so that the energies of the healee's disease can move through you and into the earth, which is closer to the healee's vibratory rate than is Source. The earth will then absorb the diseased energies and transmute the energies from used to vital.

An important part of staying grounded is to keep the chakras in the bottoms of your feet open so that the energy can flow from Source through you, into the healee, and then out into the earth through you again.

Steps to ground yourself

☆ Start the energy flowing out of your right foot and into the earth. Imagine the energy creating a half circle under the earth that arcs back into the left foot. The arc will be about 8 inches under the ground. This is enough to transform the energy, and this will touch zero chakra.

☆ Imagine tree roots coming out of your right foot into the earth. Imagine tree roots coming from the earth up into your left foot.

☆ Imagine the moon underneath your right foot, and the sun under your left. Both the sun and the moon will handle the energies for the highest good of all concerned.

☆ Imagine a roaring river flowing out of your right foot and carrying debris with it. Imagine a geyser of pure spring water coming into the bottom of your left foot.

☆ Imagine time flowing out your right foot, and the present connection to NOW flowing up your left.

☆ Imagine a rainbow flowing through your hands and heart. Create the rainbow in metals (each color of the rainbow, in this exercise, has a metallic value) coming from the earth and up your left foot. The rainbow leaves the right foot in pure light. In different parts of your body, the rainbow will take on the characteristics of Water, Fire, and Air (all Elements are represented between entering your right foot and leaving your left).

Maintaining the field

Cleansing is the process of moving energies out of the field by thought, breath, or movement. When you are connected to Source, the thought "clear this space of used energies" is enough to center the forces and energies. If the energies feel thick and/or shaky, take a deep breath in through your nose, imagining yourself pulling the air directly from above your crown chakra, exhaling it through your mouth. Any movement of the healer's hand or body will push used energies outside of the field.

Rounding is the method of taking the edges off the field as the healing progresses. As more and more used energies are driven out of the body of the healee, they tend to collect at the edges of the field, especially when they are moving rapidly. This is the moment when the healer can move the used energies out of the healing field.

The healer, in an easy and gentle manner, compacts the healing field energies as the healing progresses. This can be accomplished by peeling off layer after layer from the outside of the field like an onion. Another method of doing this is by compacting the field's purest forces and energies with statements such as, "May Source grow stronger and more compact." You may think this or speak this, and your intention will get the message to spirit. Call on the highest good of all concerned to keep the light and power from Source at the greatest intensity. This keeps the energy moving and the healing in the wave.

Grounding is the process of staying with your feet on the ground and, most importantly, with the chakras in the bottoms of your feet open so that the energies can flow in the bottom of the left and out the bottom of the right. This energetic exchange with the earth is very important, because most of the physical plane disease in the body is very heavy energy, and the flow will naturally go to the energy that is the closest in vibration.

Once you start to file most of this information into the subconscious and practice it consciously for a while, your higher self will take over and start to do these things automatically.

Chapter Eight

Preparing Statements for Healing

In preparation to be the conduit for the healing energies of Source, you must prepare to connect to Source in the strongest possible manner.

There are as many ways to connect to Source as there are people on this planet. I strongly suggest that you create a statement (affirmation or prayer) of your intention, and that you begin each healing session with this statement. When you use the same opening statement to Source each time, it increases in power.

Opening statement

Here are some guidelines for writing your statement:

☆ Make sure you and Source (God, Jesus, Buddha, or your choice) are mentioned in the same sentence.

☆ State your intention to heal.

☆ Use all positive words (*healthy*, *vitality*, *at-ease*).

☆ Make a statement about the greatest good for all concerned.

☆ State it in the NOW time.

☆ Memorize it.

"May Source come through easily and powerfully to create health in this person NOW, for the highest good of all concerned."

Key statements

Creating a key statement brings you back into the moment and to the original purpose of the healing.

The key statement I suggest is, "Gently, easily, and quickly."

Energetic statements

There are other statements that will work to facilitate healing; as you practice your healing techniques, the words will come to you at the correct time and in the correct energy. Examples include:

☆ I am a conduit for Source.

☆ The highest quality of healing energy passes through me.

☆ The clearest light passes through me.

☆ I am connected to Source.

☆ An abundance of healing energy is in use.

☆ Health is our Divine right.

Healing With Energy

☆ Let go and let God.

☆ Energy follows thought.

☆ You are one with Source.

☆ Free will gives us access to all choices in life.

☆ A direct flow is available.

☆ Receive, reperceive, and resolve.

☆ Miracles are our birthright.

☆ We are one with Source.

☆ We are totally responsible for our reality.

☆ We create our reality.

☆ The purpose of challenge is to keep us on purpose.

☆ I am one with Source.

☆ There are an abundance of healing energies present.

The statements you make serve as reminders to keep the healing in perspective. When you use the statements, they prevent you from getting caught up in the healee's issues and remind you that your job is to hold the appropriate space for healing to occur.

Chapter Nine

Ending the Healing Session

The completion of a healing is simple and direct when you pay close attention to what is going on with the healee. Completion is knowing when the healee cannot handle any more energy, or when the energy from Source has done as much as it can for that session.

Knowing when to stop

The healer must stay fully in the NOW and firmly grounded to realize when it is time to stop directing energy from Source into the healee. Your awareness of where the healee is in his or her process increases with experience. If you do not have the experience, you will need to pay extra attention as the healing continues in order to recognize when the healing session is complete.

Sometimes when healers get out of the way to allow Source to enter, they leave their bodies and do not stay grounded enough to sense when the healee has received all the energy that he or she can handle. At times, the healer may not pay enough attention to the wave, and mistakes a trough as being completion for the healee.

There are some signs that the healee has handled as much energy as possible, including:

☆ The healee's eyes are bloodshot.

☆ There is a distinct breath release from the healee.

☆ The energy from Source has stopped moving into the healee.

☆ The bottoms of the healer's feet are burning.

☆ The healer becomes dizzy.

☆ There are droplets of sweat on the upper lip of the healee.

☆ Hives appear on the healee.

☆ Any bleeding, fainting, or accidental urination occurs from the healee.

☆ Extreme shaking by the healee.

Closing the session

When the healing is complete, it is essential to close. Closing seals the healing into the aura so that the healee can most effectively and efficiently integrate the shifts that occurred during the session. It also disconnects the healer from the healee. Closing should be done while running no energy. If you run energy during a closing, you will create an ongoing continuation of the current session rather than disengaging from the healee's energies and preparing the healee to depart from the session.

Here are some techniques for closing:

Wipe

1. Wipe the energy from the heart down.

2. Wipe the energy from the heart up.

Fill with a color

1. Put your hands lightly on the person's shoulders, running no energy.

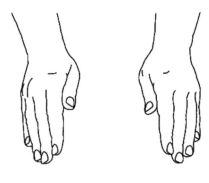

2. Quickly have the thought of one of the following colors:
    - ☆ White—to protect and seal.
    - ☆ Purple—for spiritual assistance.
    - ☆ Blue—for revitalization.
    - ☆ Green—for healing and balance.
    - ☆ Yellow—for clarity and intuition.
    - ☆ Orange—for co-creation energies.
    - ☆ Red—for activity.
    - ☆ Pink—for lightness of being.
    - ☆ Peach—for self-esteem.
    - ☆ Pearlescent—for spiritual interaction.

Fill with an essence

The purpose of "fill" is to add an essence that the healee needs and takes with them. You can fill with a primary essence; however,

Healing With Energy

choose carefully when you close someone with an essence. The essence has to be in line with the healee's path, and is not necessarily what they want. As a healer, it is your responsibility to discern the difference between the *wants* of the healee and the *needs* of the healee. This discernment will come with experience.

1. Put your hands lightly on the person's shoulders, running no energy.

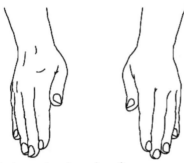

2. Quickly have the thought of an essence. Some of the primary essences are:
☆ Bliss.
☆ Wisdom.
☆ Trust.
☆ Wealth.
☆ Truth.
☆ Light.
☆ Peace.
☆ Value.

Secondary essences end in *y, ing, ness, ion,* and *ly.* The rule of thumb is that primary essences are more encompassing than secondary essences. Primary essences are the pure energy, while the secondary essences are primary essences with a modifier added to them—this diminishes the pure power of the primary essence. It is not advisable to fill with a secondary essence. To fill someone with understand*ing* limits him or her. Fill him or her with *wisdom* instead. To fill with wealth creates a powerful foundation for wealth within the healee. Modifying wealth by adding a *y* to it (wealth*y*) diminishes the power of the essence.

Wrap-up

Before the healing session, we asked the four questions to our client. After the session, there are questions we can ask to help the healee change his or her patterns so that he or she does not continue to create the disease in his or her life.

Ask

☆ What was your payoff for this disease?
☆ Why did you create this disease?
☆ What is it that you were not handling?
☆ How are you going to handle this energy now?

Please note that these questions are in the past tense except for the last one. This is done to give the healee the knowledge that the disease is not in the same state as before the healing.

Cleansing the healer

The purpose of cleansing is to make sure that none of your energies mix with the energies from Source and the lingering energies from the healee.

As a healer, there are several things you can do after closing the healing and after the healee has left. This is to ensure that you do not gather the used energy of the healee, which resonates with you. This will ensure good healer hygiene.

These are simple processes, such as:

☆ Wash your hands.

☆ Blow your nose.

☆ Go to the bathroom.

☆ Go outside to connect with the earth.

☆ Air out the room.

☆ Drink a glass of fluid.

☆ Shower or bathe.

☆ Change your clothes.

There are several exercises and visualizations to use as a way to cleanse:

☆ Form your hands into a cup linked together below your solar plexus. Then, calling on your higher power and Source, pull the energy straight along the chakra line, up over the top of your head until you touch the back of your neck. When you become clear, you will have goose bumps or chills. Continue doing this until you have them.

☆ Imagine a shower of crystal-clear light washing down from Source over you. As this shower washes you, see a puddle of used and colored energies at your feet.

☆ Breathe in Source through your crown. With each breath, blow out through the chakras, one by one, all the energy that is not like light. Start with the third eye and move downward. One breath per chakra is usually sufficient. Less is more.

☆ Let your guides and angels cleanse you. Wait until you feel the chills before starting. They will do what it takes.

☆ Click your fingers in front of all your chakras. Then, starting out from your heart, click seven times to clear the subtle body.

☆ Imagine the notes of *do, re, me, fa, so, la,* and *ti* reso-
nating outward from the subtle bodies, until the
sound vibrates away all the used energies.

> *Coming to completion with the healee and ensuring
> that you cleanse your own field afterward are
> critical to both you and the healee.*

Part Two:

The Healer's Toolbox

The Healer's Toolbox:
Introduction

In Part One of *Healing With Energy*, you learned about the many foundational aspects of being a healer and gained an understanding of the important Elements at work during the healing session. Each time you make an addition to your healer's toolbox, whether the tool is used or not, it gives the healer more knowledge about working with energy, and of the various healing processes. When you work with energy in a new or different way, this adds to your understanding of the healing process; it also adds to your knowledge of how Source works.

You will not use all of the techniques in *Healing With Energy*; however, I do recommend that you try each at least three different times on three different types of healees so that you will capture the essence of the technique.

Processes of healing

The overall process of healing can be simple and easy, or it can be complex and complicated; it depends on the attitude of the healee and the skills of the healer. To know what the process is composed of is to understand the cause of the disease, and your ability to respond to that cause.

The basic process of healing is being a conduit for Source to the healee. The healing may take a long period of time even with the healer connected to Source with a strong intention to heal. The speed of the healing depends on the attitude of the healee and their willingness to move through their "stuff." The quality of the healing depends on the ability of the healer to stay in NOW time and maintain the connection to Source.

As with any other healing technique, the laying on of hands can be improved upon if the healer and the healee are informed. Some of the information the healer needs is made available in this manual. The healee also needs to be informed while the healing is in progress, as well as before and after the healing.

Encouraging the healee

One of the most valuable things a healer can do is encourage the healee to take responsibility for his or her own healing. It is not the position of the healer to work harder than the healee in the healing process. If this is happening, I encourage you to stop and explain to the healee that you are working harder, and if he or she would like the healing to continue, he or she is required to put more energy into the process.

Encourage your healee to take deep, full breaths. When the energy is about to shift, the healee may hold his or her breath or swallow. This is the pattern fighting to stay in the healee. Gently, tell him or her to use the breath to let go of the "used" energy.

The importance of breathing cannot be stressed enough.

When the healees are far too still, ask them to shake off their hands or to move their feet so that the energy can shift and start the process of moving outward. You may want to ask questions of the quiet healees, and may want to tell the talkative ones to use their energy to heal rather than to chat.

Source makes the call

All processes you will use will take on a life of their own. Similar to a new mother nurturing a baby, you need to observe and care for the healee until the healee becomes more experienced at the healing process. In the beginning of a session, each movement has significance, so *do not close your eyes*. Source can easily flow through you with your eyes open. The movements of the healee give you clues, along with the opportunity to observe how the healee takes the energy into the body and how the body uses or resists the energies. This is the point where your subconscious mind will receive the information to determine what technique is to be used. You do not decide *before* you put someone on the table that you are going to use a certain technique. The technique will be known when the flow of energy from Source calls for it.

Sometimes you will be moved to do things that may not seem normal or may appear to be very strange. Stay in the NOW and do them without questioning. Sometimes Source will alter a technique or process to get more efficient use out of the energy flowing through you. Listen.

Use all of your heavy and light senses. At times, the room or the healee may feel heavy or cold. You may smell odors as the energies are being let go by the physical body of the healee. Out of the corners of your eyes you will notice movements as energies float or zoom off the healee. Do not get caught up in the phenomena; stay in the NOW and continue to be a conduit for Source. In cases where there is a major amount of energy removed, pictures may fall off the walls or you may hear loud noises. When this happens, *do not* take your hands off of the healee. Extraneous things can wait to be taken care of after the session ends.

Get a sense of the flow of energy through the healee. Follow the wave and support yourself. You are the one who changes the radio channels while Source is the electricity.

The importance of the right energy

There are times when the healee is very serious, and the healing process seems heavy. Step into the healing energy in your heart. The power of love to lighten a situation is incredible. Notice whether your face is serious, and smile to give the energy the quality of lightening up. Feel the connection that healing gives you with all humans. Let this roll over you and fill you to the brim.

Session review

After the healing it can be beneficial to run through the thoughts that were in your head. Sometimes these thoughts, which seem random, are directly from Source and can add to your general knowledge of healing. The thoughts can also give you insight as to where the healee needs to be worked on next time.

As slow as possible, review your movements and the way that the energy moved in your mind. As Source comes through the healer, techniques will be given as needed. If you find yourself doing some things over and over again, notice what they are.

These movements may vary a little from healee to healee, yet they will have a flow of their own. Sit down and document the sequence and the circumstance of the healee. Later, you may find techniques similar to different materials that are put in your path.

In Part One, you read about the key concepts in a healing session. Use this list to refresh your memory:

☆ As a healer, you serve as a conduit for the healing energies from Source.

☆ Maintaining a clear connection with Source is critical.

☆ Keep your ego out of the way.

☆ Source and the healee are doing the work.

☆ Respect free will.

☆ Get permission.

☆ Drop your judgments.

☆ Identify the type of healee you are working with.

☆ Ask questions and discern truth.

☆ Ask Source to do the healing gently, quickly, and easily.

☆ You will not always be able to give the healee what they want; sometimes you will give them what they need.

☆ Stay centered in the healing field, grounded and using your breath.

☆ Identify which light sense you are using.

☆ Use your understanding of the Four Elements.

☆ Use your statements.

☆ Know the moment of completion.

☆ Close and cleanse.

☆ After the session, review and make notes.

Heal together

Remember, as you heal others, you are also being healed. Check in with yourself and sense where the change has occurred. Each healee is directed to you because you also have something similar to heal in yourself. You as the healer have handled what the healee is going through, and you still have a bit more to handle in that particular vibratory aspect.

The process of healing is one of the greatest spiritual acts that humans can do together; each healing is whole and complete in its essence. Any judgment you may have about the healing is an indication that you still have more to learn about healing and yourself. Anything that you say or judge about the healee is something that you personally need to hear and work on in a lesser degree than the healee. Observe your thoughts and words. Learn from yourself as well as others.

To truly be complete is to be one with Source, healee, and yourself. This means asking that every action, thought, and energy in a healing session be for the highest good of all concerned. When you enjoy doing something, it is easier to do. Enjoy being a healer. Time passes quickly when you love what you do. Use your time and energy wisely.

Most importantly, walk your talk!

The Healer's Toolbox:

Exercises

The following exercises are useful in developing your skills, foundation, and sensitivity as a healer. They are also very effective ways to tune into and connect to the energies of the healee. Remember that as the healer, you are a conduit from Source. The real healing occurs between Source and the healee. The more you can tune into the energies of the healee and at the same time connect to Source, earth, and your own inner self, the more powerful and effective the healing energies will be. Some of these will become things that, after some practice, you automatically do during a healing without thinking or judging what you are doing. Each person and experience you have as a healer adds to your personal healing toolbox.

In any healing that you do, it is recommended that you first cleanse, ground, and connect. To cleanse, you may choose to use any of the exercises listed in the cleansing section of this book, or you may choose to use a favorite cleansing technique that is not listed in this book. The same applies for grounding. Use one of the grounding techniques in this book, or use a favorite grounding technique that you have learned elsewhere.

After cleansing and grounding, there are three more connections to make before beginning the session:

1. To Source.
2. To your own inner self.
3. To the healee.

To connect to Source, please refer to one of the techniques listed in this book for connecting to Source, or choose a favorite technique that is not mentioned in this book. To connect to your own inner self, simply bring your attention to the space within you behind your heart chakra. See, feel, or hear yourself in that space, and simply check in as to where you are at this moment. Connecting to the healee is very quick and easy once you complete these other steps. All you need to do is say some words of greeting to the healee, touch the healee, and let your healee know that you will now begin the session.

Knowing hands

1. Cleanse, ground, connect.
2. Reach out and touch healee wherever your hands are led.

3. Disconnect your hands from yourself.
4. Allow your knowing hands to move on their own.

Earth touch

1. Cleanse, ground, connect.
2. Imagine your hands are the warmest of earth.
3. Knowing hands.

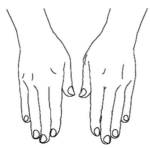

4. Imagine that your hands are the coolest of earth.
5. Knowing hands.
6. Alternate until you sense completion.

Faucets

1. Cleanse, ground, and connect.
2. Imagine that your hands are faucets.

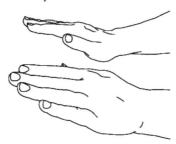

3. Imagine hot water moving through your hands.
4. Knowing hands.

5. Imagine cold water moving through your hands.
6. Knowing hands.
7. Alternate between cold and hot water until you sense completion.

Hot and cold

1. Cleanse, ground, connect.
2. Knowing hands.

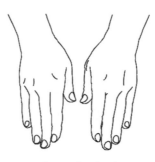

3. Sense the energy from the healee.
4. Where energy is hot, run cool energy through your hands.
5. Where energy is cold, run warm energy through your hands.

Net

1. Cleanse, ground, connect.
2. Imagine a net between your hands.

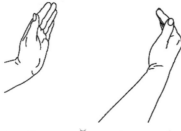

3. The space between the strands of the net is microscopic.
4. Imagine the net is connected to your hand chakras.
5. This net is constructed of the strongest healing light.
6. Pull the net through the toxic areas of the body and dispose of energy by shaking it off of your hands.
7. Use different colored light nets as needed. If you sense that a colored light is needed, employ that.

Push-pull

Whenever there is excess energy in the healee's body or any of the healee's subtle bodies, this technique is very beneficial. It is also beneficial for noticing and filling in areas where the healee needs more energy.

1. Cleanse, ground, connect.
2. Knowing hands.

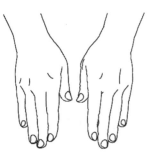

3. Sense any areas where the energy is either pushing out from or pulling into the healee.

4. When energy pushes, pull.

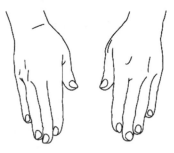

5. When energy pulls, push.

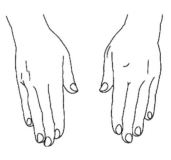

Sponge

1. Cleanse, ground, connect.
2. Imagine that your nondominant hand is a sponge.

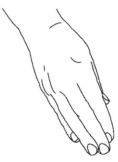

3. Wherever toxins are present, tune in.
4. Imagine that the toxins are magnetized to sponge.
5. When the sponge gets heavy, give it to Source.

6. Create a new sponge in your hand and continue the steps until toxins that are ready to leave have been eliminated.

Vacuum

1. Cleanse, ground, and connect.
2. Knowing hand (dominant).
3. Imagine that this hand is a vacuum.

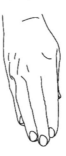

4. Pull out used energy.

5. Let go of the energy through dominant hand.

6. Properly dispose of the used energy.
7. Fill voids with light.

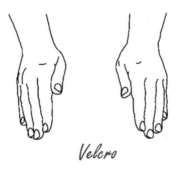

Velcro

1. Cleanse, ground, connect.
2. On both hands, create a magnetic vital charge.
3. With intention, let the magnetic charge pull unvital energy to it.

4. This acts like Velcro.
5. When sticky, dispose of the Velcro appropriately.

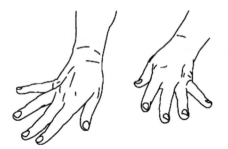

6. Create more Velcro and continue until you sense completion.

Wind tunnels

1. Cleanse, ground, connect.
2. Imagine that your hands are wind tunnels.

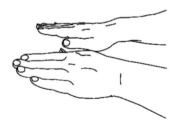

3. Imagine warm, strong air coming from your hands.
4. Knowing hands.

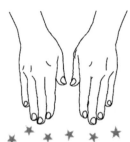

5. Imagine cool, strong air coming from your hands.
6. Knowing hands.
7. Alternate between cool and warm air, as needed.

The Healer's
Toolbox:
Breathing Techniques

During a session, the air that a healer exhales is filled with used energies from the healee. Sometimes, it is wise to use breathing techniques to rid the healee of his or her used energy. During a session, when there is a large amount of devitalized energy let go by the healee, you may find it helpful to use your breath to move the devitalized energies out of the healing field.

Doggie breaths

Use doggie breaths when the devitalized energies in the healee are formed into small, broken chunks. This technique provides the energy with a ragged, small chunk that is easily let go of.

1. Cleanse, ground, connect.
2. Knowing hands.

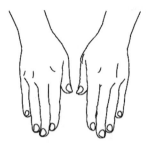

3. Both hands on body with nondominant hand on "spot."
4. Fill with the appropriate primary essence using your dominant hand.
5. Bring energy up to your lungs with your nondominant hand.

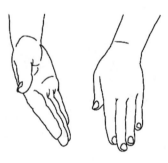

6. Open your mouth and pant like a dog.

Fire breath

Use fire breath on healees who appear very white and are holding on tightly to a pattern. Healees who complain that they are cold, and the ones who lay too still, will greatly benefit from the use of fire breath. Have water available for you and the healee to drink, because fire breath will dehydrate both of you.

Note that the use of fire breath on healees who are red in the face, have an abundance of body heat, or have high blood pressure is NOT recommended.

1. Cleanse, ground, connect.
2. Knowing hands.

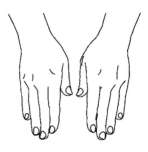

3. Place your dominant hand on "spot."

4. Keep nondominant hand off of the healee.
5. Place tip of your tongue slightly above your top teeth.
6. Feel the heat.
7. Breathe the heat in and out.
8. Direct heat downward and out of your dominant hand into the healee.

   Warning: Use with awareness and caution.

Power breath

Power breath is a beneficial technique when there is an abundance of devitalized energy to be moved out of the healee, *and* it is not in the form of chunks.

1. Cleanse, ground, connect.
2. Knowing hands.

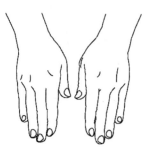

3. Put both of your hands on the healee's body with nondominant hand on "spot."
4. Fill the spot with energy from the dominant hand.
5. Pull the devitalized energy up to your lungs with your nondominant hand.

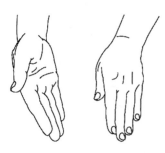

6. Purse lips, and with focused breath let go of the healee's devitalized energies.
7. Repeat until "spot" is clear.

Healing With Energy

Water breath

Water breath is to be used with the healee who has to have control. Healees who talk a lot during the session will benefit from water breath. Sometimes it works well with the resistors, and sometimes it adds to their resistance. With practice, you will be able to identify the healees who will benefit from this technique.

Note that the use of water breath on an alcoholic, bleeder, or a healee who has an infection, bladder problems, or urinary problems is NOT recommended.

1. Cleanse, ground, connect.
2. Knowing hands.

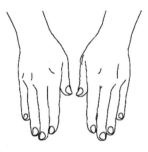

3. Place dominant hand on "spot."

4. Keep nondominant hand off of the healee.
5. Place your tongue on the roof of your mouth.
6. Feel the water.
7. Breathe the water energy in and out.
8. Direct the water energy downward out of your hand into the spot on the healee.
9. Repeat until the healee stops talking and relaxes into the healing.

Use an abundance of water to clear out any resistances.

The Healer's Toolbox: General Techniques

he purpose of these general techniques is to control the type of energy that flows into the healee. Techniques will fine-tune, smooth, and alter the energy, so that the different parts of the body receive energy in forms that are appropriate to raise the level of vitality.

The techniques we will cover vary from simple to complex multi-person energy exchanges.

The African healing circle is used to remove thought forms from the body.

1. Start by creating an imaginary circle about a foot in diameter above the area horizontal with the thought form, and use both of your hands to form the circle.

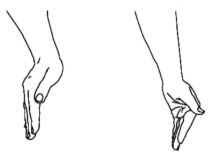

2. With your hands facing each other, start to gently push the circle together with energy and hand motions until it is smaller.

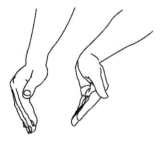

3. Make sure that your hands touch and tuck the thought form, compacting it more and more, gradually lowering it until both of your hands are touching the healee's body.

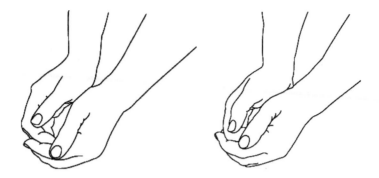

4. Now, start to use physical pressure, and squeeze your hands together, still using energy to compact the thought form.

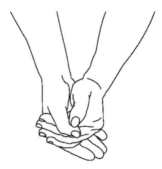

5. Keep compacting until one of your hands encircles the other.

6. When you feel that you have a firm grip on the thought form, quickly pull upward and slap your hands together to send the thought form to Source.

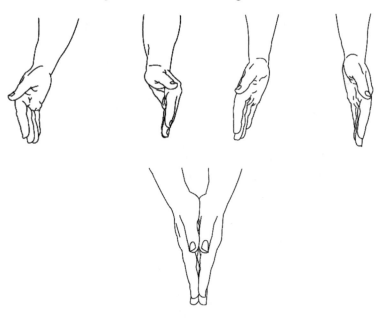

Chakra-balancing techniques

The chakra is a receptor and a vortex that receives, perceives, and filters energies from you, and the world around you. When you subconsciously or consciously choose to deal, or not to deal, with energies, you choose whether your chakras will be healthy, vital, malfunctioning, or will shut down. There are six chakra-balancing techniques covered in this book.

Element balance

The element balance calls the Elements to the chakras, so you can fill the chakra with the Element that it is lacking. This

Element will be what the chakra most needs. The Elements provide different tools for the chakras and subtle bodies to use during the healing process.

1. Each of the following fingers corresponds to an Element:

Thumb: Earth

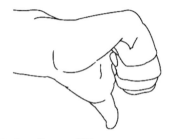

Index finger: Water

Middle finger: Fire

Ring finger: Air

2. About 3 inches above the chakra, starting with the crown, test the energy with all four fingers. One of your fingers will respond with a different energy. Fill this chakra with the Element, calling on the Element with intention, while pointing that finger at the chakra.

3. When you get to the root chakra, pause and cleanse yourself, then start the same process, testing with your fingers upward to the crown. Maintain a 3-inch distance from the chakra.

4. The amount of time that you spend filling each chakra will vary, and when you pay attention, you will know when to stop. The average time for a nonchronic is about six minutes. Time for a chronic dis-eased person varies, and could take as long as 24 minutes when done correctly.

Long stroke

This is the most time-consuming chakra balance. Use this technique when you want to use a deep and very thorough chakra clearing and balancing.

1. Start by grabbing the feet.

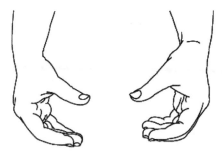

2. Focus on the root chakra and imagine the subtle bodies above it. Start at the top of the body and look for oil slicks, holes, rough spots, and tears. Do this very slowly. Ask the soul and higher self of the healee to use Source coming through you to mend, repair, clean, and straighten this part of the layer. When the subtle body feels or looks strong and together, check it again, and move down to the next level, covering all seven layers.

3. Repositioning your body, move in a clockwise direction and repeat when you are positioned at the right-hand side of the healee, with your hands on the healee's body.

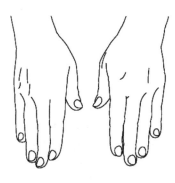

4. Repeat at the crown.

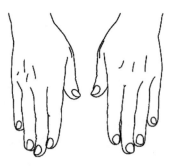

5. Repeat at the left side.

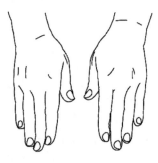

6. Each time, touch the healee with both hands and work with Source to clear and repair the layer of the auric field on which you are working.

7. When you get back to the feet of the healee, you can now start the rest of the balance. Holding on to the feet, pull in Source directly to the healee, starting with the crown chakra, pulling the energy all the way through the root chakra.

Warning: Because this energy is coming directly from Source to the healee, it should not go through you.

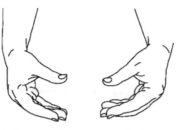

8. Ask the higher self to control this part of the process, and use you to stop and start. This is the part of the exercise in which you will not touch the healee. You will guide the higher self by saying "now" when the chakra is filled with light.

Quick pop

1. This is a quick and easy chakra balance that can be used any time you would like to clear the current devitalizing energies that are in the chakras.

2. Form a fist with the thumb touching the middle finger.

3. Relax the fist so that there is a small opening all the way through the hand. Make the opening small enough for air to flow through, yet not big enough to see a lot.

4. You will be doing this technique, starting with the root chakra and moving upward, popping each chakra, and finishing with the crown.

5. For the root chakra, the fist must be perpendicular to the ground and between the legs as close as possible to the root without being crowded by the thighs. Cup your other hand and make three passes in the air over the opening. On the fourth pass you will gently, yet quickly, pop the top of your closed fist. This should make a noise.

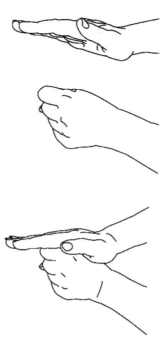

6. Chakras 2, 3, 4, 5, and 6 are done perpendicular to the chakra. Start at the crown or at the root, and move in order through the rest of the chakras.

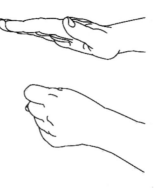

Healing With Energy

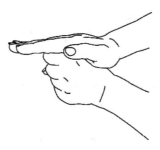

7. The crown chakra is done perpendicular to the top of the head.

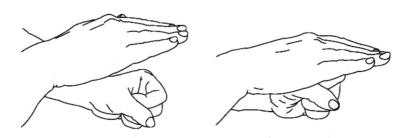

8. This chakra balance tucks the etheric bodies to the chakra and loosens debris in the chakra to facilitate it leaving the chakra area.

Super charge

The super charge is to be used on healees who have stress or physical exhaustion. It is *not* to be used on dis-eased people or on healers.

1. Hold your right hand facing the heart chakra and your left hand cupped with its back touching the back of your right hand (hand chakras back to back).

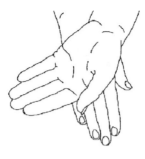

2. Begin by pulling the color of the heart chakra (green) slowly, and increase the speed of your pull so it is pulling at light speed when you finish.

3. The closer the right hand is to the chakra, the more power the light will carry. Watch the energy carefully, and start pulling with your hands away from the body so as to not overload and create an imbalance.

4. Balance the heart first, and then choose whether to go upward or downward to the next chakra. Go upward if the person is too grounded or serious, then when you finish the crown, go to the solar plexus and move downward to the next chakra, repeating the steps above, and using the appropriate chakra color. If the person operates from the mind, start at the heart and move downward, coming to the throat and moving upward after the root.

Three breaths

1. This is a simple exercise to be done along with the healee. Have the healee breathe in from Source and breathe out of the chakra.

2. Do this three times for each chakra. Match your breaths with those of the healee as both of you breathe light in and used energy out.

3. Do not touch the healee, but stay as close in his or her aura as possible.

Triangle balance

The triangle balance is a great overall chakra balance. It is more thorough than the quick pop, and less thorough than the long stroke.

1. Each chakra should have a triangle visualized over it in the color of that chakra. For Earth-based chakras, put your hands on the healee's body below that chakra about 12 inches apart and, in your mind, form the triangle to have the chakra in its center.

2. For spirit-based chakras, put your hands on the healee's body about 12 inches apart and situate them so that the chakra is in the middle of the triangle.

3. Start at the root and work upward, staying with each chakra until you feel complete.

First: Root—red, base to earth

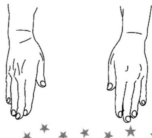

Second: Sacral—orange, base to spirit

Third: Solar plexus—yellow, base to earth

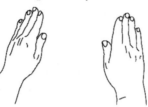

Fourth: Heart—green, base to spirit *and* base to earth

Fifth: Throat—blue, base to spirit

Sixth: Third eye—purple, base to earth

★ ★ ★ ★ ★ ★ ★ ★ ★ ★ ★ ★ ★ ★

Seventh: Crown—white, base to spirit

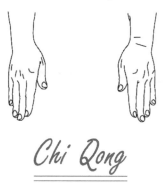

Chi Qong

Chi Qong quickly relieves pressure energies and pain. Use it anytime, anywhere, and any place. It is easy and simple.

1. Cup both hands, making sure the thumb runs along the side of the hand and ends up resting on the index finger's side.

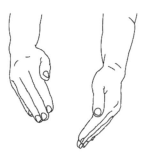

2. Place cupped hands about 3 to 4 inches above the healee's body.
3. Start making random patting motions in the air.
4. Each hand works independently.
5. The hands should constantly change directions, angles, and speed.

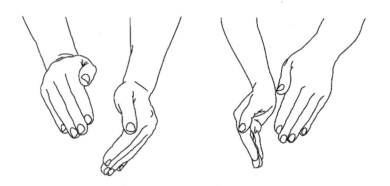

6. Do this for about four minutes.

Clockwise spiral

Use this technique to open or loosen the flow of energy. It will also soften constricted muscles, relieve pinched nerves, remove congestion, and relieve arthritis. Do NOT use this on bleeding or on any open wound because this technique will exacerbate the bleeding.

1. With this technique, you will use a variety of specific parts of the hand, for specific purposes:

☆ **Indicator finger:** Use this finger for very narrow and specific work. This looks like a soft laser beam if you do not push the energy. Be gentle.

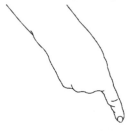

☆ **First and second fingers:** This is focused and general energy. In several techniques you will use these two fingers to move energy. After you choose which part of your hand to use, follow the steps following the images.

☆ **Hand chakra:** This is used in situations where the energy is very tight; that is, stress, grief, and situations with excess tension.

☆ **Full hand:** Use this with children and babies, because the full hand has a secure, calm, and nurturing effect.

2. Direct the energy with your dominant hand.
3. Make clockwise circles that spiral.
4. Make the circles about three times the size of the area you are healing.

5. Stay about 2 inches away from the body.
6. While continuing to make circles, move outward slowly to about 16 inches.
7. Repeat for a total of three times.

Comb

If your healee needs to get fluids moving in the body, using the comb will start clearing out the devitalized energies through the bodily fluids. This technique works with the body's fluids and penetrates cavities such as the sinuses and lungs. Sometimes it is very helpful to move the fluids in the stomach and intestines.

1. Place nondominant hand on body.
2. Spread your fingers apart on dominant hand.
3. Start to comb the aura about 2 to 4 inches above cavity.

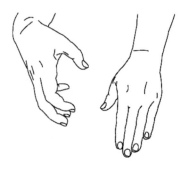

4. Clear hand.

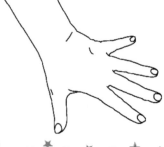

5. Repeat several times until you sense that the fluids are flowing in the body, and the devitalized energies have been removed.

Counterclockwise spiral

1. Use counterclockwise motions to close down energies such as warts, bleeding, infections, and fungus. The counterclockwise spiral is an unwinding energy; therefore, do *not* use on broken bones. This technique closes down excess energy. Be aware of what you are shutting down when you use this energy.

☆ **Indicator finger:** This is a laser-like energy and needs to be used in small places when doing very fine work.

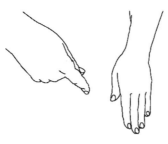

☆ **First and second fingers:** This is a softer energy and is generally used when doing the counterclockwise technique.

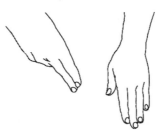

☆ **Hand chakra:** This is used when the energy is very loose, such as fainting and so on.

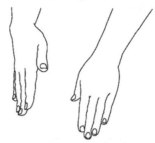

☆ **Full hand:** Use this energy with small children, especially at bedtime.

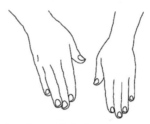

2. Place nondominant hand on the healee.
3. With your dominant hand, make spiral-shaped counterclockwise circles.
4. Make the circles about three times the size of the healing area.
5. Stay about 2 inches away from the body.
6. Move outward to about 16 inches.
7. Repeat three times.

Creator's sphere

This is to be used with new pain, aches, and discomfort. This technique is not effective in removing old pain.

1. With the middle finger and thumb of the dominant hand, form the letter *C*.

2. Imagine that these fingers are holding a small planet Earth with the vivid blue and green colors of azurite and malachite.

3. In a right to left direction, start the Earth rotating on its axis.

4. Insert the rotating sphere into the affected area of the healee's body as you continue to hold on to it.

5. As your hand gets heavy, itchy, tingly, or grimy, toss the sphere away.

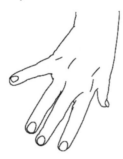

6. Keep replacing spheres until the healee remarks on the difference in the area.

Eyes

This exercise will improve the vision. Do it to your healee for 28 days in a row, and he or she will see 100 percent better. Do not touch the healee.

1. With the healee seated, stand behind him or her.
2. Form your hands into an *L* shape.

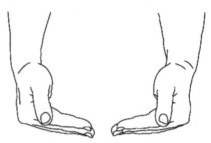

3. With your hands in front of the healee's eyes, touch your fingertips.

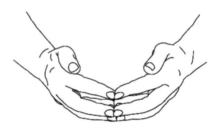

4. Pull your fingers apart about a quarter of an inch.
5. The healee should keep his or her eyes open throughout the process.
6. Start your fingers moving in a wave-like motion from top to bottom.

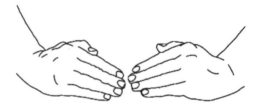

7. Leave enough space between your fingers so that you break up the light going into the eyes of the healee.

Healing With Energy

8. When you feel the energy collect in your hands, let it go by shaking your hands off; repeat this process.

9. Cup your hands over the eyes of the healee and visualize a wave of energy passing through your hands. The healee should keep his or her eyes open.

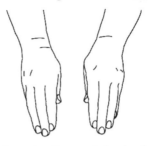

10. Walk around to the front of the healee. Place your hands over the healee's eyes while neither sending nor receiving energy.

Flood

The flood technique will fill spaces with "new" energy, creates vitality, and will circulate to add to existing energies. Sometimes you will intuit the need to flush before flooding.

1. Place right "knowing hand" on body.

2. Use left hand to pull energy from Source.

3. Flood body with energy through right hand.

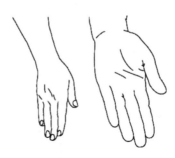

Flush

Use the flush to drain "used" energies from the body, start toxins flowing, or to move the supporting energy out from under a block or thought form.

1. Place left "knowing hand" on body.
2. Begin to pull energy out.
3. Ask Source to filter.
4. Hold right hand out.
5. Ease "used" energy out of right hand.

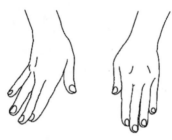

6. Follow this technique with a flood, or another filling technique.

Four directions

Four directions is a Native American technique. It can be used on any place on the body. It is especially effective on joints, ligaments, and tendons. It fills the area quickly with energy.

1. Knowing hands.

2. Place nondominant hand on healee.
3. Place dominant hand on top of your other hand.

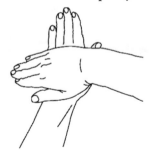

4. Starting in any of the four directions, fill the spot with energy.
5. Going clockwise to the next direction, place your dominant hand perpendicular to its last position and fill.

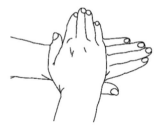

6. Do this until you have completed all four directions.

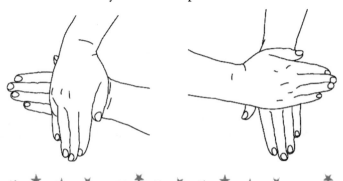

7. Balance other side of body if necessary.

Four Elements and four directions

1. Use the same technique as described previously. In each position, bring through the Elements in this order:

    ☆ 1. Air
    ☆ 2. Fire
    ☆ 3. Water
    ☆ 4. Earth

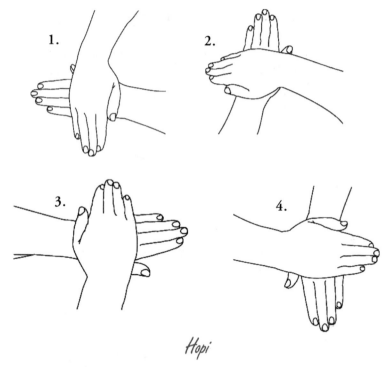

Hopi

Hopi is a technique that is used to fill a healee with energy. Use it when the healee is drained or uncomfortable. Hopi is exceptional for people who have a chronic disease, because his or her body needs more energy to continue the healing process.

Do these steps 11 times:

1. The healee is lying on his or her stomach.
2. Position dominant hand over nondominant hand, with the hand chakras over each other.

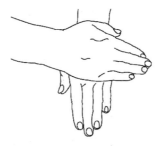

3. Place hands on the back, where the heart chakra is.
4. Fill with vitalized energy. You will know when to stop filling.
5. Keeping nondominant hand on back of heart chakra, form dominant hand into a laser gun using your first and second fingers.

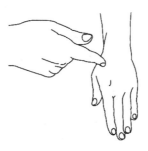

6. Emit a beam of energy into the back of your other hand on the healee. Stir in clockwise circles.

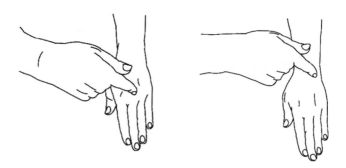

7. You will know when to stop.
8. With your middle fingers and your thumbs, form a *C* shape. All other fingers will point straight out.

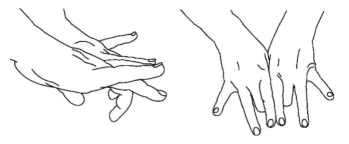

9. The mouth of the *C* encompasses the spine. The fingers sticking straight out let go of the collected energy from the back of the heart chakra.

10. To seal, place nondominant hand on the back of the healee's heart chakra, with your dominant hand touching so that the hand chakras are aligned. At this moment, do not send or receive energy—you are sealing. This action should be quick.

Long-distance healing

Many healings can be effectively done from a distance. The light energy that you bring through during any healing session will move faster than the speed of light, so it will reach the healee anywhere on the planet in less than a second. The quantum physics at work during a long-distance healing session often shorten the amount of session time (as the energies are delivered in a more compact form), compared to a traditional one-on-one healing session.

1. Cleanse, ground, connect.
2. Breathe in, finding the vibration of the person.
3. Find the wave of the person.
4. Raise the vibration.
5. Adjust the wave.
6. Let go of the vibration.

Pullouts

Pullouts are techniques that pull out energies from the bodies. These are usually done with quick and rapid movements. The most important thing to remember about pullouts is that the energy holding the block or thought form needs to be loosened in order to pull the devitalized energy out.

The clap

1. Knowing hands.

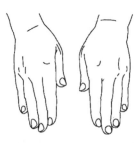

2. Fill area with energy and wait for major shift in energy.
3. Draw devitalized energy outward.
4. Clap suddenly and quickly.

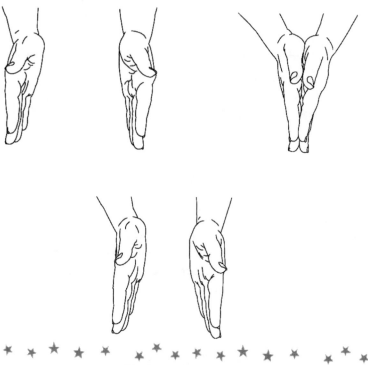

5. Check to make sure energy dissipated.
6. Fill the area from which you pulled out the energy with the appropriate colored light.

The draw

1. Knowing hands.

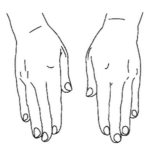

2. Fill area with energy.
3. Notice the shape and size of the block or thought form.
4. Grab the devitalized energy and hold firmly while gently pulling it away from the body.

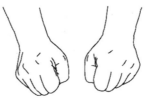

5. Dispose of the energy properly.

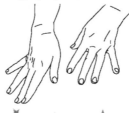

6. Check to make sure area is clear.
7. Fill area with the appropriate colored light.

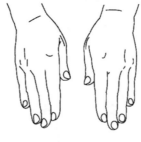

The hook

1. Knowing hands.

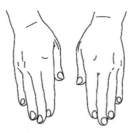

2. Fill area with energy.
3. Wait until you feel a shift in devitalized energy.
4. Hook with your finger and quickly pull out energy.

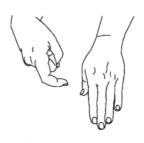

5. Dispose of properly.

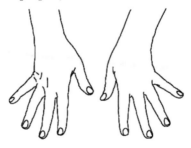

The snap

1. Knowing hands.

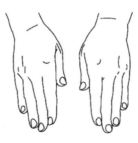

2. Fill area with energy.
3. Wait until you feel the energy shift.
4. Place hand between 2 and 4 inches from the body.

5. Snap fingers quickly three times.

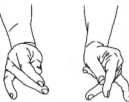

6. Fill area with vitalized energy.

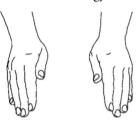

Surrogate healing

Sometimes you will want to do a more detailed long-distance healing. This is where it could be beneficial to use a surrogate. When using a surrogate, remember to work with someone who is in fairly good health. While it is not necessary, you may choose a surrogate to facilitate the healing who has similar characteristics (physically, mentally, emotionally, and/or spiritually) to the healee.

1. Cleanse, ground, connect.
2. Ask permission from the surrogate if you can use his or her body to heal another.
3. Ask the healee for permission to heal him or her through the surrogate.
4. Notice the change in the surrogate's energy.
5. You may notice a buzzing, snapping, or clicking sound as the shifts occur.
6. Find and raise vibration.
7. Find and adjust wave.

The picture

The picture is a technique where the healer and the healee work together to change the picture of a disease. When you use this technique, you and the healee will use energy together to make changes.

1. Place your hand on the healee's shoulders.

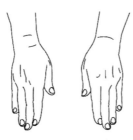

2. Start by asking these questions (ask healee to answer each question before moving to the next):
   ☆ Where is the disease?
   ☆ What size is it?
   ☆ What shape is it?
   ☆ How much does it weigh?
   ☆ What color is it?
   ☆ What texture is it?
   ☆ What does it sound like?
   ☆ What does it feel like?
   ☆ What does it smell like?

3. These questions will start the process of *consciously* separating the disease from the healee. Make sure that he or she answer each question completely, because answering the questions will let the healee become more familiar with the disease.

4. With this technique, the healee actively participates in his or her healing. He or she will be able to play and add more of his or her own energy to the process than with most techniques and exercises.

5. Bring one of the following active visualizations into play. This will add energy to the healing by adding sound and color. Keeping the answers to the original questions in mind, give the healee a choice between two of the following:

☆ **Pac Man:** Imagine tiny Pac Man creatures eating away at the edges of your disease. Chomp, chomp, chomp. See how busy they are? Feel the disease getting smaller. Listen to them at work. You and the healee make "chomp" noises together. Now speed up the sound.

☆ **Laser Gun:** Imagine that you have a laser gun. This laser gun shoots the purest healing energy and light. Start shooting the disease. Make laser gun noises with the healee. See the disease getting smaller. Hear the noise as it breaks apart and dissolves. Feel the difference. Speed up the laser gun noise.

☆ **Waterfall:** Imagine that a huge waterfall, such as Niagara Falls, is flowing through the disease. The waters are full of healing energies. Make water noises with the healee. See the water washing away the disease. Feel the force of the waters. Hear the water. Speed up the water noises.

☆ **Flamethrower:** Imagine that you have a flamethrower. This flame is the flame of purification. Shoot the disease. You and the healee make flame noises. See the flames working. Hear the flames. Feel the difference in the diseased area. Speed up the flame noises.

☆ **Tornado:** Imagine that you have control of a tornado. This tornado is of the winds of light. Have the tornado whip through the area of the disease. You and the healee make tornado noises. See the tornado whipping away the disease. Hear the tornado at work. Feel the difference in the disease as the tornado works. Speed up the tornado sounds.

☆ **Jackhammer:** Imagine that you have a jackhammer that will break up the disease. Have the jackhammer start on the edge of the disease working inward. You and the healee make jackhammer noises. See the jackhammer working. Hear the jackhammer. Feel the difference in the disease as the jackhammer works. Speed up the jackhammer noises.

☆ **Vacuum Cleaner:** Imagine that you have a vacuum cleaner that sucks up disease. Have the vacuum cleaner start at one edge of the disease. You and the healee make vacuum-cleaner noises together. See the disease getting smaller. Hear the vacuum cleaner working. Feel the difference in the disease. Speed up the vacuum-cleaner noise.

☆ **Lawn Mower:** Imagine that you have a lawn mower. This lawn mower mows away the devitalizing energy. Have the lawn mower start at one edge. You and the healee make lawn-mower noises. See the disease getting smaller. Hear the lawn mower at work. Feel the disease lighten. Speed up the lawn-mower noise.

☆ **Bubbles:** Imagine bubbles that clean. These bubbles clean used energies and leave the vitalized energies. Have the bubbles start at all the edges of the disease. You and the healee make bubble noises. See the bubbles working. Hear the bubbles at work. Feel the disease getting smaller. Speed up the bubble noises.

☆ **Mr. Clean:** Imagine a friendly Mr. Clean dressed in white. He cleans up used energies. You and the healee make noises of cleaning brushes at work. See how strong he is and how hard he is working. Hear the brushes at work. Feel the used energy disappearing. Speed up the noise of the brushes.

6. After doing the visualization, ask the healee these questions:
   ☆ How do you feel?
   ☆ What size is the disease?
   ☆ What shape is the disease?
   ☆ What texture is the disease?
   ☆ What is the difference in the disease?
   ☆ What does it have to say to you?
   ☆ What does it need to know to leave?

   The healee should tell the disease to answer. Ask if the disease needs anything else.

7. If the disease does need something else, then the healer works with the healee to address that need.

8. Now, choose a second tool from the visualizations and use it until disease is gone. To make up your own tool, include sound, sight, and feeling. Make noise with the healee. Work for a few minutes then speed up sound. Keep checking until the disease is gone. Give the same process to the healee as homework.

The pulse

In certain parts of the body, the pulse plays an important part in healing. We are going to start simple and work our way up to advanced. This is very important: the universal healing rate is 72 beats per minute.

1. Place your hand on the healee's body.

2. You are going to feel pulses that are different in quality and intensity when you use healing energy. These are the pulses on which you will focus:

   ☆ **Strong pulse:** This feels like a drum or a small fist. This is usually associated with an organ that is not riding the energies of the wave and needs healing.

   ☆ **Rolling pulse:** This is a muscle pulse; you can feel the pulse rolling away from the healing energy of your hand as the muscle absorbs the energy.

   ☆ **Pinpoint pulse:** This is a tiny pulse that is about the size of a pin and indicates a nerve that needs alignment.

3. When you feel the healing energies from Source activate these parts of the body, you will notice the pulse, and whether that pulse is slow or fast. It is not important to count. You will know when the pulse is at 72 beats per minute.

4. Sometimes it helps to make this statement: "Subconscious mind that is there to serve and protect, I ask you to serve now by adjusting the pulse to 72 beats per minute."

5. Ask the subconscious to take Source's energies into itself for the highest good of all concerned.

Tuck

This technique will take the edge off and concentrate the body's natural healing energies to support healing. It gives ease to the healee. It is also a great pain reliever.

1. Start at about 6 inches out from edge of healing area.
2. Tuck the energy like a pie crust.

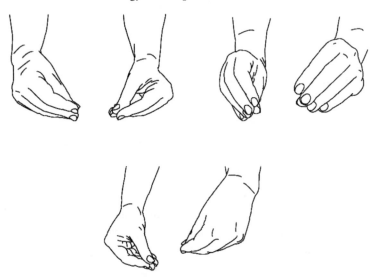

3. Make sure you go all the way around area.
4. Pat around and fill with blue light.

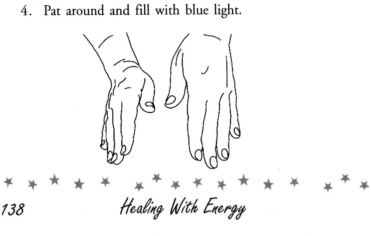

5. Fill with green light.

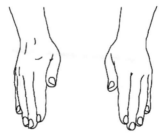

The Healer's Toolbox: Emotional Healing

The difference between feelings and emotions is that feelings are in NOW time. Feelings serve an important purpose in our lives, and they are part of our growth and healing; it is essential to learn how to express them appropriately. Emotions are feelings that have not been dealt with or appropriately expressed. They carry with them charges that relate to our reactions to past events. Emotions, when not dealt with, will sit in our cells and auric fields, becoming denser and denser with time, as more and more emotions are added to them. Eventually, these repressed or suppressed emotions can turn into a physical disease.

As a healer, your role is to assist the healee in accessing and letting go of repressed and suppressed emotions, which have been stored in the healee's cells and field.

Anger buster

This technique is excellent for helping the healee let go of suppressed and repressed anger.

1. Cleanse, ground, connect.
2. Place dominant hand under left armpit.
3. Place the other hand on back of neck.

4. From back of neck pull anger out.

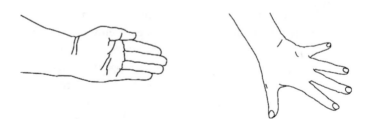

5. Fill the armpit with green energy.

6. As the anger loosens, the call for green will become strong.
7. Shake off nondominant hand and place on neck.

8. Pull anger out.

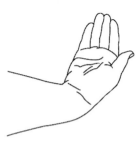

9. Fill the armpit with blue energy.

10. Repeat steps one through nine until you feel completion.

11. Shake off your hands.

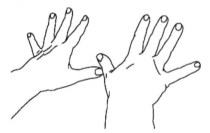

12. If anger isn't moving, do the quick pop chakra balance exercise from pages 107–109.

13. Without touching the healee, pop the back of the neck chakra.

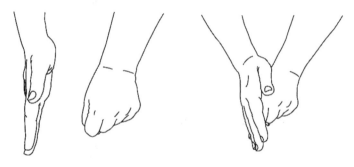

14. Repeat the quick pop chakra balance exercise.
15. When anger stops, do the quick pop.

Clear head

When a healee is in a state of confusion, the clear-head technique disconnects the suppressed or repressed emotional patterns from the healee's thought processes.

1. Cleanse, ground, and connect.
2. Place dominant hand on head.
3. Place nondominant hand on back of neck.

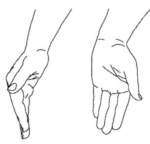

4. Run yellow energy through crown chakra.
5. Run green energy through crown chakra.
6. Run blue energy through crown chakra.
7. Run white energy through crown chakra.
8. Repeat the process after about 10 minutes.

Cradle of the heart

If the healee is suffering from a lack of nurturing, especially if this is rooted in the child/mother experience, the cradle of the heart will reprogram the heart energies to bring in the wholeness created with nurturing.

1. Cleanse, ground, connect.

2. Place nondominant hand below left rib cage.

3. Direct the energy toward the heart.
4. Keep hand still until the healee's heart has taken in a sufficient amount of energy.
5. Move energy in cradle motions.

6. Used energy will leave.
7. Cleanse hand frequently.

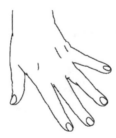

8. Repeat often, until you sense a feeling of wholeness and well-being in the healee.

Deep heart

When the healee is at the point of getting ready to let go of deep-seated, long-term wounds and emotions, this technique is highly effective in filling in the areas of the heart that are most in need of support.

1. Cleanse, ground, connect.
2. Place nondominant hand in middle of chest and make sure it is at heart level.
3. Place dominant hand on back.

4. Make sure hands are across from each other, with the healee's body in between.
5. From hand on chest, send gentle green energy.
6. From hand on back, send gentle pink energy.
7. Alternate between green and pink energy.
8. Repeat several times, until you sense that the energy is complete.

Grief relief

When the healee has held on to grief for a long period of time, grief relief is an excellent technique for letting go. If the healee starts to cry during the technique, it is recommended that the healer stop using this technique, and move to something else.

1. Cleanse, ground, connect.
2. Place nondominant hand on heart.

3. Gently pull grief from heart. Shake off hand.

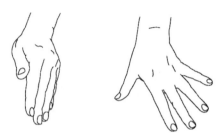

4. With dominant hand, fill heart with pink energy.

5. Place nondominant hand on solar plexus.

6. Gently pull confusion out of chakra.

7. Fill solar plexus with clear yellow energy.

8. Put hand on third eye.

9. Pull separation out of third eye.

10. Fill third eye with white light.

11. Place hand on crown chakra.

12. Fill crown with peace.

13. Brush off healee's shoulders.

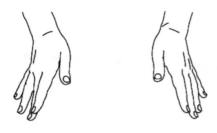

14. Open up chakras in bottom of feet.
15. Use clockwise circles.

16. Open up hand chakras.
17. Use clockwise circles.

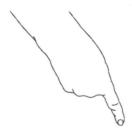

Puffed heart

When the healee is challenged by a lack of the ability to give or receive love to self and others, puffed heart will fill the healee's heart with love, reminding the healee what love is.

1. Cleanse, ground, connect.
2. Place dominant hand under left rib cage.

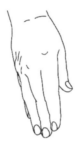

3. Send "puffs" of unconditional love.
4. Send straight pink energy into heart.
5. Send puffs of unconditional love.
6. Send straight green energy.
7. Keep alternating.

White heart

When the healee has disconnected his or her head from the heart, the white heart technique serves to reestablish the flow of this connection. This technique is excellent for healing the physical heart and for maintaining a healthy heart.

1. Cleanse, ground, connect.
2. Lay healee on the floor.
3. Check to see which way the heart energy is flowing.
4. Place hands on or over chest with thumbs meeting creating a *W*.

5. The finger part of your hand should be over the nipples.
6. *W* points up to head.
7. Sense if energy is moving up to head from heart.
8. Reverse the *W* so that it points to feet.

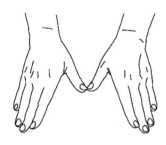

9. Send energy to head of the healee.
10. Cleanse, ground, connect.
11. Kneel at the head of the healee.
12. Place hands on top of each other.
13. Make sure your hand chakras are aligned.
14. Rock forward, pushing at the heart energy.

15. Do this several times.

16. Go to the left shoulder and kneel.
17. Place hands on the physical heart.

18. Put energy into the heart.
19. Slowly lift energy upward.

20. Redirect the heart energy.

21. Repeat until you sense completion.

Wide heart

When the healee's heart energies are in a state of restriction or limitation, wide heart will open up and widen the healee's heart energies so that he or she may fully experience his or her emotions.

1. Cleanse, ground, connect.

2. Place both hands on side of chest.

3. Make sure hands are at heart level.

4. Send gentle pink energy from left to right.

5. Send gentle green energy from right to left.

6. Keep alternating.

7. Keep the aura clean above heart.

8. Keep alternating.

It is important with this technique to sense if energy is moving from the heart toward the feet. Some people will put their heart energy into their head, while others will use their heart energy to support the needs of their body. If the heart energy is flowing up or down, it is not in the best interest of the healee, because the heart energies are meant to reach out to others and the world. If the heart energies are not open to reaching out, the healee will continue to experience difficulties in relationships with himself or herself and others.

In cases where the energy from the heart is subtle, it may be necessary to put your hands on the chest of the healee. Make sure you and the healee are comfortable with this, because this is a sensitive area.

Wide sinuses

When the healee holds on to repressed and suppressed emotions, and it shows up in the tension of the healee's face, this technique will clear the emotions held in the face. A healee may cry during this technique. It is important *not* to pat the healee while he or she is crying. Allow him or her to experience this emotion, as you hold the position.

1. Cleanse, ground, and connect.
2. Place hands on face.
3. Thumbs should meet between brows.

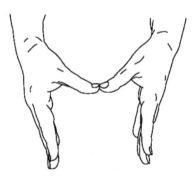

4. With hand chakras, send Water energy into the face.
5. Send Air energy into face.

6. Send blue energy into face.
7. Repeat until the healee has expressed emotion or the tension in the face softens.

Affirmations

Affirmations are lies that we keep telling ourselves until they come true. For an affirmation to truly be effective, it is essential to be familiar with the concept of *frequency* versus *intensity*. A lack of understanding of this concept can cause an affirmation not to work.

You may have an affirmation that you say every morning when you get up. You put all of your feeling and intensity into this affirmation, and you shout it out to the world. You have used intensity in the expression of this affirmation. Then you go about the rest of your day and think a thousand things that are the opposite of the affirmation you said that morning.

Which thoughts will create your reality? Right…the thoughts that you think most frequently.

It is *frequency* not *intensity* that causes an affirmation to work, so it is critical that when you use, think, and say your affirmations, you do those things considerably more than you would think opposite, critical, or sabotaging thoughts, which created your old pattern.

There are several ways that you can provide your healee with homework. Frequency is a critical element with affirmations, as is identifying an affirmation that resonates with the healee. In this section, you will find many examples of affirmations for specific physical, emotional, mental, and spiritual healings. You may provide your healees with these, or work together with your healees to help them create their own affirmation. Remember to keep the affirmation in the present moment.

☆ **Appendix:** I speak words of strength.

☆ **Arm:** I am able to handle life with love.

☆ **Arteries:** I have a powerful flow of life.

☆ **Asthma:** Freedom is my birthright.

☆ **Back:** I support my choices and myself.

☆ **Bladder:** I gently release my hold with ease.

☆ **Bleeding:** My understanding is permanent.

☆ **Blood:** I accept the flow of life through me.

☆ **Blisters:** I respect my body's state.

☆ **Bones:** Life treats me in a graceful manner.

☆ **Bone Marrow:** I have purpose in life and living.

☆ **Bowels:** I change my thinking and keep actions flowing.

☆ **Brain:** I accept the presence of all thoughts now.

☆ **Breast:** I lovingly nurture my desires with strength.

☆ **Bronchial Tubes:** I accept life by breathing easily now.

☆ **Bursitis:** I use the proper tools for all jobs.

☆ **Buttocks:** I get up and go clearly.

☆ **Calluses:** There are many ways to Source.

☆ **Calves:** My ability to move and act is energized now.
☆ **Cancer:** All my cells grow normally.
☆ **Cataracts:** My vision of the future is clear.
☆ **Cartilage:** My purpose is connected to my actions.
☆ **Cellulite:** My thinking process moves forward.
☆ **Cerebral Palsy:** I correct my actions gently.
☆ **Cheeks:** I express my emotions kindly.
☆ **Chest:** My love is limitless.
☆ **Circulation:** I understand my responsibilities.
☆ **Collar Bone:** Healthy dignity and self-worth are mine.
☆ **Colon:** I absorb vital energies only.
☆ **Congestion:** I change my limitations to free myself.
☆ **Constipation:** I release the past now.
☆ **Crotch:** My privacy is whole and intact.
☆ **Cuts:** I am full of care.
☆ **Cystic Fibrosis:** My direction and goals are on target.
☆ **Depression:** My attention is on what is.
☆ **Diabetes:** I have plenty to give.
☆ **Diarrhea:** I have plenty of time to complete.
☆ **Dyslexia:** I am receiving what is valuable.
☆ **Ears:** I listen with discernment.
☆ **Earache:** I listen to my inner self.
☆ **Elbow:** I am flexible within.
☆ **Emphysema:** I am responsible for fulfilling my desires.
☆ **Endometriosis:** I express my feminine energies powerfully.
☆ **Epstein Barr:** I act on my desires of purpose for existence.
☆ **Esophagus:** I receive information easily.
☆ **Eye:** I perceive and see clearly to understand.
☆ **Fainting:** I support learning.

☆ **Feet:** I move toward progress with understanding.

☆ **Fever:** I am cool about growth and expansion.

☆ **Fingers:** I grasp, handle, and hold my activities.

☆ **Fungus:** Others respect my boundaries.

☆ **Gall Bladder:** I gently process all energies.

☆ **Genitals:** I am pleasured by my sexual energies.

☆ **Gingivitis:** I pay attention to details about myself.

☆ **Glands:** I direct my growth and development lovingly.

☆ **Growths:** I dissolve my conflicts unconditionally.

☆ **Gums:** I am absorbing my experiences daily.

☆ **Hair:** My sensitivity adds to my vitality.

☆ **Hand:** I enjoy handling my activities.

☆ **Head:** I accept all thoughts.

☆ **Heart:** I accept the love force now.

☆ **Heartburn:** I make progress in life lovingly.

☆ **Hemorrhoids:** All my thoughts are gentle and timely.

☆ **Hepatitis:** My life's details are sacred.

☆ **Hernia:** I live wisely with creativity and desires.

☆ **Herpes:** I am secure in my identity.

☆ **Hiatal Hernia:** My attention is on processing data now.

☆ **Hips:** My adjustments create self-support.

☆ **Huntington's Disease:** With feeling I create purpose.

☆ **Hypoglycemia:** All I have inside is valuable to others.

☆ **Hypothyroidism:** I am mentally active.

☆ **Ileocecal:** Everything new adds to my experience.

☆ **Impotence:** I respond strongly to all situations.

☆ **Indigestion:** I pay attention to what is in front of me.

☆ **Influenza:** I quickly and easily make my decisions.

☆ **Ingrown Nail:** I have proper perspective on life.

☆ **Insomnia:** I release attention from my thoughts and relax.

☆ **Intestines:** I let go and accept my inner needs as good.

☆ **Jaw:** I am objectively focusing and concentrating.

☆ **Joints:** My hold on life is flexible.

☆ **Kidney:** I process criticism so that I grow.

☆ **Knees:** I am humble.

☆ **Laryngitis:** I complete my desire to speak.

☆ **Leukemia:** The world is my playground.

☆ **Legs:** My ability to move forward is unlimited.

☆ **Lips:** My feelings and words are one.

☆ **Liver:** Constructive energies are my way of life.

☆ **Lungs:** I am inspired by life and love.

☆ **Lupus:** I let go and let God.

☆ **Lymph Glands:** My defenses are strong, mobile, and quick.

☆ **Melanoma:** My image of myself is pleasing.

☆ **Migraine:** I control only myself.

☆ **Mouth:** My power of expression is pure.

☆ **Mucus Membranes:** I face life clearly.

☆ **Multiple Sclerosis:** I run toward learning.

☆ **Muscles:** I express my strength powerfully.

☆ **Nails:** Source protects my energy flow.

☆ **Narcolepsy:** I am stimulated to learn.

☆ **Neck:** I communicate my creative expression.

☆ **Nerves:** I receive and direct life's experiences clearly.

☆ **Nose:** My perceptions are communicated.

☆ **Ovaries:** My maternal instincts are fulfilled.

☆ **Pancreas:** My acknowledgements are frequent.

☆ **Paralysis:** All my movements are acceptable.

☆ **Parkinson's Disease:** I participate in experiences of life.

☆ **Pelvis:** My entire world accepts support.

☆ **Piles:** I choose my choices gently.

☆ **Plantar Wart:** I make decisions promptly.

☆ **Prostate:** My masculine powers are potent.

☆ **Psoriasis:** I express my opinions.

☆ **Rectum:** I release my waste practically.

☆ **Rheumatism:** Mentally I move forward easily.

☆ **Ribs:** I receive enough energy to support my personality.

☆ **Scars:** Consciously, I resolve my stress.

☆ **Scoliosis:** I reveal my true identity to all.

☆ **Shingles:** I allow change to flow through my life.

☆ **Sinus:** I gently release my self-expression.

☆ **Skin:** I express my emotions and feelings.

☆ **Sores:** I heal outside and inside quickly.

☆ **Spleen:** My being copes and protects me easily.

☆ **Stomach:** I digest my processing.

☆ **Stroke:** My body accepts all conditions of my life.

☆ **Tailbone:** I maintain my survival energies.

☆ **Teeth:** I use all parts of my life.

☆ **Tendons:** My energy flow is smooth and graceful.

☆ **Thighs:** I support and fulfill my desires.

☆ **Throat:** I express creativity, power, and self.

☆ **Thrush:** I am responsible in the ways I influence others.

☆ **Thymus:** I understand and accept my maturity.

☆ **Thyroid:** I use my will in a vital manner.

☆ **Tinnitus:** I listen to the thoughts from self.

☆ **Toes:** I participate in playing and fun.

☆ **Tongue:** I say what I want expressively.

☆ **Tonsils:** Authority nurtures me.

☆ **Tumors:** All hate turns to love inside me.

☆ **Ulcers:** I stay in the NOW.

☆ **Urinary:** All guilt turns to forgiveness in me.

☆ **Varicose Vains:** My flow of love is constant.

☆ **Vomiting:** I assimilate my experiences in order easily.

☆ **Womb:** I nurture my feminine role.

☆ **Wrinkles:** I express my timeless beauty with joy.

☆ **Wrist:** I am flexible with my work and purpose.

Glossary

A

Absent Healing: This process of healing involves the healer projecting healing energy through time and space, and is directed at a person or group not physically present in the room with the healer. Also known as *distant healing* or *remote healing*. See *Projection*.

Acupressure: A healing technique that involves the surface stimulation of various acu-points of the Chinese meridian system and specific energy channels that run through the body. These points are energetically stimulated manually or with handheld tools.

Acupuncture: This ancient Chinese medical system was recently revived in China and is now becoming popular in the West. Acupuncture focuses on the balance of yin and yang energy. It helps to regulate the flow of *chi* (subtle energy) throughout the meridian system, and when the chi is balanced, the human body's health is restored, and disease is eliminated or managed. During acupuncture, the practitioner inserts fine needles at key pressure points along the meridian system for varying periods of time to establish appropriate flow throughout the meridians. Acupuncture has been used in surgery as a substitute for anesthesia. See *Chi, Meridian, Yin and Yang.*

Acute Illness: A disease with an abrupt onset and usually short in duration. See *Chronic Disease, Disease,* and *Healing Crisis.*

Affirmation: Affirmations are lies that you keep telling yourself until they become true. They are positive statements—either spoken, written, or thought, of both outcome and intent—that help the mind concentrate on what an individual wants to be true. The process of repeating affirmations can facilitate the manifestation of these missing or desired outcomes and intents into one's life.

Air Element: This is the quickest, gentlest, and easiest Element for a healer to use. Good for beginning healers. Air knows how to get in through the smallest opening. It seems to carry vitality and allows the body's natural healing functions to activate. Used energy is absorbed by Air and quickly carried out of the energy system. The lower subtle bodies also use Air to remove the devitalizing energies. The main side effects of using Air to conduct energy from Source through a healer is that the healer or healee may burp, yawn, sneeze, or flatulate often. See *Earth, Fire,* and *Water Elements.*

Akashic Records: These records are sometimes referred to as the Universal Mind in which everything is stored. Information about every soul is contained there. The Akashic Records are the indelible record of all events and all knowledge that is part of the Cosmic Consciousness. Everything that has already happened or anything that will come to pass is stored in the Akashic Records.

Alchemy: The chemistry of the Middle Ages focusing on changing the base Elements into gold. Metaphorically, it refers to spiritual transformation.

Alpha Wave: Brain waves associated with a relaxed, alert consciousness. See *Beta Wave* and *Theta Wave*.

Amulet: An object charged with personal energies through a ritual or meditation, which is then used for protection in order to ward off a certain force or person. See *Low Magic*.

Angel: Spiritual beings portrayed especially in Persian, Jewish, Christian, and Islamic theologies. These beings are typically depicted with wings and portrayed as messengers of God. They can act as spiritual guides for individuals, however Angels cannot intervene of their own accord; the individual is required to ask them for help. See *Guide*.

Angry: Painfully inflamed. All emotional feelings of anger are signals that there is something in life that needs to be dealt with. When anger comes up, it is a signal that something in life is out of balance and incongruent with how an individual believes their world should be. See *Rage Work*.

Anthroposophical Society: Spiritual movement founded by Rudolf Steiner in 1912, which emphasized biodynamic gardening and farming as well as Christian Theosophy.

Aromatherapy: A type of herbal medicine that uses the essential oils from plants, flowers, herbs, and trees to promote health, vitality, and rejuvenation of the body, mind, and spirit. See *Essential Oils*.

Ascended Masters: Realized souls from various esoteric traditions who no longer exist on the earth plane.

Astral Body: A subtle body that is created in the image of the physical body, and which travels, works, and plays on the astral plane. See *Subtle Bodies*.

Astral Plane: A plane parallel to the physical world and traveled through by the astral body during astral projection.

Astral Projection: This is the experience, whether spontaneous or induced, of traveling through the astral realm in the form of the astral body. Also known as astral travel.

Atomic Healing: Healing at the level in which the atomic structure of a person's being is shifted or transformed.

Attention: Focus of energy. Energy flows where the attention (and intention) goes.

Attunement: Aligning the individual with the natural energy in the environment to be in harmony with natural laws.

Auditory Modality: NLP (Neuro-Linguistic Programming) learning style of auditory perception. People who operate from this modality learn by what they hear. Healers who operate from this modality receive information through clairaudience, messages, and sounds they hear. See *Clairaudience* and *NLP*.

Aura: This is a subtle, "invisible" essence or fluid that emanates from all things, living and nonliving. It is an electromagnetic field creating a force field that is made up of a complex combination of ingredients including atoms, molecules, and energy cells. As these ingredients coexist, they generate a large magnetic energy field that can be sensed, felt, and even seen around the physical body. The aura is the part of our soul that we wear on the outside of our body. See *Endomorphic Energy* and *Soul*.

Ayurveda: This ancient Hindu medical/metaphysical healing science is based on the harmony of body, mind, and Universe through diet, exercise, herbs, and purification procedures. It emphasizes the capability of the individual for self-healing using natural remedies to restore balance. Allegedly, Ayurveda is the most complete system of natural medicine and the mother of all healing arts. Also known as *ancient indian medicine* or *vedic medicine*.

B

Bardo: The afterlife reality through which we travel as we process our life review, confront emotional situations, and confront unfinished business to see if we have sufficiently let go of the seeds of karma so we can be freed from their influence. See *Karma*.

Base Chakra: First energy center located at the base of the spine. This chakra is the center of survival and deals with our survival on the physical plane, as well as our physical health and vitality. It is associated with the color red and the musical note C. See *Chakra, Seven Chakra System,* and *Twelve Chakra System.*

Beta Wave: Brain waves indicating a normal waking state with consciousness directed toward the external environment. See *Alpha Wave* and *Theta Wave.*

Bilocate: To be in two or more places at once through the use of higher consciousness techniques. At the same time the physical body is in one place, the exteriorized spirit body is present at a distant place.

Biofeedback: A learned technique for consciously controlling biological processes. Amplified brain waves are monitored through the use of an electronic device that feeds information back to the practitioner, who then helps train the healee to create different reactions.

Biorhythm: Science studying changes in a person's emotional, mental, physical, and spiritual states based on 23-, 28-, and 33-day cycles, which are calculated from the date of birth.

Black Magic: Magic that is *against* something, therefore giving more power to the *other* side. There are also karmic repercussions for black magic. Think of the "against" energy as a "butting" energy, antagonistic, a clashing of forces. It looks for the negative. "What you resist, persists." More is accomplished with *white* magic. When we are against something, we give more power to the other person (what we are against), and there are karmic repercussions. See *High Magic, Magic, Low Magic, Middle Magic,* and *White Magic.*

Breath: This is the air that a person takes in and expels from the lungs. In a healing, this is the air that comes from a healer as the healer breathes, which is filled with used energy from the healee. Sometimes it is wise to use the breath to rid the healee of their used energy.

Button: A personal issue that triggers a strong reaction. See *Core Issue.*

C

Caught Teaching: Information received by the subconscious/unconscious mind from another person's aura. The subconscious mind is capable of processing 10,000 bits of information per second. See *Initiation* and *Taught Teaching.*

Causal Plane: Highest plane of existence, also called *Sivaloka* or *Karanaloka.* It is the world of gods and highly evolved souls.

Cellular Healing: The specific focus of healing energy to the cells of an organ, system, or bodily fluid. Cellular healing works with the universal law "as above, so below." In metaphysical logic, if the cells are healed, the organ or system will also heal.

Centering: Remaining in the center of the energies and force. See *Grounding.*

Chakra: A chakra is a portal that funnels electromagnetic energy into and out of the body. It is identified by a spiral vortex that vibrates at a specific hertz. There are seven main chakras located on the torso beginning in the groin area and extending upward to the top of the head. Another five of much higher vibration exist in the extremities and the auric field. Unlike the main chakras, these higher chakras do not all spin in the same direction. Each of the seven main chakras is strategically located to nourish and regulate specific vital organs and areas of the body. Each also serves to stabilize specific emotional and psychological states. Every chakra channels a particular quality of energy that can be identified by its color and vibration. The seven comprise the naturally occurring color spectrum array of a rainbow—red, orange, yellow, green, blue, purple, and white. In addition, the vibration of each chakra has a specific pitch, comparable to musical notes from A to G. See *Seven Chakra System* and *Twelve Chakra System*.

Channeling: A process that is often used by psychic and healing channels to receive energy or information from a spirit or entity. The difference between a medium and a channel is that the medium accesses the emotional and astral planes for this information, and the information obtained from this plane can be convoluted. A channel accesses a higher level of information. See *Medium*.

Charge: Energy that sparks an emotional reaction, generally triggered by an unresolved issue. See *Emotions* and *Core Issue*.

Charismatic: One of the five light senses. This light sense keeps letting us know that there is more to know and do in a situation. It keeps us fascinated in the healing process and interested even in the most boring times. Charismatic energy lets us know that there is an answer. Often, the healee will change his or her life after a few words from a charismatic healer. See *Electric, Electromagnetic, Magnetic,* and *Presence*.

Chelating Energy: The process of a healer running energy in such a way that it bounces back and forth between the healer's hands.

Chi: (Chinese) Universal life energy. See *Acupuncture*.

Christ Consciousness: A term the Christian tradition has used for intuitive knowing or the realization or attainment of high consciousness. It refers to the pure level of consciousness in which the mind, love, and will of God are made known to the enlightened person. This consciousness is characterized by the color gold. See *Enlightenment*.

Chronic Disease: A disease that persists for a long period of time (three months or more). See *Acute Illness* and *Disease*.

Clairaudience: Extrasensory data is received from the emotional and astral planes by this auditory light sense and perceived as sound.

Clairsentience: Extrasensory data is received from the emotional and astral planes by this empathic light sense, and perceived often as physical feelings.

Clairvoyance: The light sense that involves the paranormal ability to see psychic information, including historical or future events or other phenomena that cannot be discerned naturally through the five material senses.

Clockwise Motion: A movement or direction that opens the energies.

Closing: Sealing in the healing energy at the end of a session. See *Completion*.

Clutter: Clutter takes two different forms: mental and physical. Mental clutter is made up of thoughts that continually run through the mind. Physical clutter can be found in a person's kitchen, closets, bedroom, storage areas, family room, bathroom, office, home office, as well as on calendars or planners. Physical clutter can add to our mental clutter because of the constant reminder that there are things that need to be done. The act of clearing out the physical clutter lessens our mental clutter. See *De-cluttering*.

Codependent: Codependent people have unhealthy boundaries. They are more likely to get involved in relationships with people who are perhaps unreliable, emotionally unavailable, or needy. The codependent person tries to provide and control everything within the relationship without addressing their own personal needs or desires, and these actions create an environment filled with continual frustration and feelings that something is missing. Even when a codependent person encounters someone with healthy boundaries, the codependent person will still operate in their own system; however, they're not likely to get deeply involved with people who have healthy boundaries. This results in the continual creation of recycled problems. If codependent people do not heal, it is unlikely that they will get involved with people who have healthy behaviors and coping skills, and their problems continue into each new relationship. See *Drama Triangle*, *Persecutor*, *Rescuer*, and *Victim*.

Communication: The exchange of thoughts, messages, or information through speech, signals, writing, or behavior. It also involves energetic transmissions that are perceived by the subconscious mind.

Completion: The process of completing a healing. Completion is knowing the moment when the healee cannot handle any more energy, or when the energy from Source has changed to the healee's energy. This is a simple and direct process when close attention is paid to the healee.

Conduit: A channel for energy to move from one place to another. The healer functions as a conduit for energy from Source to the healee.

Confusion: An internal battle between two deeply ingrained belief systems. Confusion is the step before enlightenment.

Consciousness: Awareness—the state of the mind, the senses, and physical awareness that allows a person to know of his or her existence, sensitivities, and relationship to environment. The most important insight about the nature of consciousness is that all individual consciousness is simultaneously collective consciousness. There is one consciousness in the cosmos: the cosmic total consciousness of which every being has an inalienable part. This consciousness is an amalgamation of the consciousness of all monads in the cosmos.

Core Issue: An unresolved issue that buries itself deep in the core of our foundation that affects a person's life at all levels and can cause physical disease. In order for a healing to be complete, addressing the core issue of the disease is required.

Cosmic Consciousness: The combined consciousness of all sentient and nonsentient beings throughout the cosmos. Through the subconscious mind, any being can tap into this consciousness for the purpose of gathering information or relating to other energies.

Councils: Groups of nonphysical light beings that serve the purpose of guiding the evolution of cosmic consciousness.

Counterclockwise Motion: Movement or direction that shuts down energies.

Crest: This is part of the wave in a healing when the energy is rising to the highest amplitude and wattage that the healee can handle. See *Energy Wave* and *Trough*.

Crown Chakra: Seventh energy center located on the top of the head. We use the crown chakra as a tool to communicate with our spiritual nature. It is through this vortex that the life force is dispersed from the Universe into the lower six chakras. The crown chakra is associated with the color violet or white and the musical note B. See *Chakra, Seven Chakra System,* and *Twelve Chakra System.*

Curandero(a): One who cures; a healer of a specific Mexican Shamanic tradition.

De-cluttering: Clearing our space and our minds of things that no longer serve us. See *Clutter.*

Dehydration: Water conducts energy, so when the healer or healee lacks the appropriate amount of water in her body, the energy does not flow as easily. See *Hydration* and *Water Element*.

Deva: In Hinduism and Buddhism, devas are exalted beings of various types. The word *deva* in Sanskrit means "shining one." Hinduism recognizes three types of devas: mortals living on a higher realm than other mortals, enlightened people who have realized God, and Brahman in the form of a personal God. In Buddhism, devas are gods who live in the various realms of heaven as rewards for their previous good deeds; they are still subject to rebirth.

Dimensional Mastery: The Curanderos work with 144 dimensions. Dimensional mastery refers to the ability to work within these dimensions and navigate the space-time continuum, letting go of perceived physical plane laws in the process. In mastering the dimensions, it is possible to walk through walls, walk on water, levitate, and teleport. See *Physical Plane*.

Dimensions: A means of organizing different planes of existence according to their vibratory rate. Each dimension has certain sets of laws and principles that are specific to the frequency of that dimension. There are 144 dimensions in the Curandero tradition.

Disease: Disease is the state of not being at ease, and not being in alignment. Disease usually involves a core issue, belief, or pattern that affects the physical body. When the core issue is resolved, the disease often dissipates. See *Acute Illness* and *Chronic Disease*.

Disincarnate Being: A being that exists without a body. Some disincarnate beings are humans who died and did not cross over to the other side. Others are here from other dimensions, here to observe and often to assist us. See *Entities*.

Distant Healing: See *Absent Healing*.

Distinction: The moment of distinction comes after asking the appropriate questions, then becoming the observer of the energy dynamics at work in the situation. Often, common words that we use every day can lose their meaning. For example, making a distinction between the use of the word *emotions* (which exist in the past) and the use of the word *feelings* (which exist in the present time) can help you ascertain if you are working in the past or in the present moment.

Divine Intervention: Divine intervention is where Source (God, Buddha, higher power) comes through, resulting in the physical and the spiritual taking action at the same instant to create a miracle. In other words, Divine intervention is the phenomena where tumors fall to the floor and/or diseases may go into spontaneous remission. Divine intervention may be referred to as the loudest, most specific prayer that can call the forces of nature and heaven together, hand in hand. The most intimate connection that one can have with another being on this planet is to hold the space for a split second, so heaven can appear in or for someone. As Source intervenes in a situation, through a minister-healer, the laws of a larger physics come into play. The possibility that the body may return to its natural state of wholeness jumps astronomically. At this moment, the physical body may surrender to be used to the fullest by Source as the electric and magnetic energies split. When this happens, anything that is not vital to the energetic structure of the body appears outside of the body, and can then be disposed of properly. See *Miracle* and *Prayer*.

Divining Rod: A divinatory tool. This is a long, narrow rod used by dowsers to gives tangible signals that answer their questions.

DNA Healing: Healing and replacing undesired DNA patterns and diseases by changing the energy blueprint of the DNA.

Dousing: The practice of locating water, minerals, or other objects through the use of a rod, pendulum, or other object.

Download: A transmission of energy and information.

Drama Triangle: The drama triangle shows the dysfunctional dramatic roles that people act out in daily life. These unstable, repetitive roles are emotionally competitive and create misery and discomfort for all players, sooner or later. The switching of roles occurs between persecutor, rescuer, and victim, which generates and perpetuates the drama and the painful feelings that occur when people with hidden agendas and secrets manipulate people and situations for dysfunctional personal advantage. See *Codependent, Persecutor, Rescuer,* and *Victim.*

E

Earth Element: The most stable and grounded Element of the Four Elements. Earth is basically composed of the energy of presence, even though all of the light energies are present in different minerals of the earth. When a healer uses earth energy consciously or unconsciously, he or she takes the disease into his- or herself and moves it out of the healee's field. See *Air, Fire, Healing,* and *Water Elements.*

East Direction: One of the four directions. A place where peace, light, and new life rise up each day. People with an affinity to the east are generally intellectual in nature. The East is the direction of blood and birth. See *Four, North, South,* and *West Directions.*

Ectoplasm: The substance that comes from specific bodies, animals, and plants, and travels through the ether and shows emotions.

Ego: Self; feeling of I, me, mine. It is man's consciousness of himself. Esoteric philosophy teaches the existence of two Egos in man: the mortal or personal; and the higher, the Divine, or impersonal (calling the former "personality," and the latter "individuality"). See *Consciousness* and *Personality.*

Electric: One of the five light senses. This is the light sense that seems to be exceptionally giving. Similar to electricity, it carries a charge. Healers that are electric seem to be busy doing and adding energies in all manners of form. This sense is responsible for our hair on our arms standing on end. When someone touches us and we jump, that is electric energy. See *Charismatic, Electromagnetic, Magnetic,* and *Presence.*

Electromagnetic: One of the five light senses. This is the light sense that evaluates the push and pull of the energy in the healee. This energy is very powerful because as the needs of the healee shift, so does the electromagnetic energy. Often, this energy can be really balanced, while at other times the percentage of electricity and magnetic energies can change significantly depending on what is coming through from Source. *See Charismatic, Electric, Magnetic,* and *Presence.*

Elohim: "Those who came from the sky." This group of beings is one of the most advanced group of light beings in the Universe. They are responsible for the generation of life on this planet and the creation of human beings on this planet. The Elohim have been involved on Earth ever since the first human was created, in a kind of genetic manipulation experiment. Throughout history, the Elohim have come to Earth at different times, to different cultures, and they heavily influenced many cultures throughout history. They were thought to be the Gods and spirits of many of the major and minor religions that continue to exist today. The Elohim heavily influenced these religions, providing a moral structure to help the people of this Earth survive successfully and viably. Therefore, when this structure didn't work, religion became instead a political influence tool to help establish order and maintain control of the population. Still, to this day, the Elohim are involved in Earthly matters.

Emanation: Using intention (thought) to send energy to be received by someone or something outside of us.

Emotional Body: The body that holds unresolved emotions and currents of force awaiting expression.

Emotional Plane: The plane of existence upon which our emotions exist, serving as messengers to provide us with information about the energies that need to be dealt with.

Emotions: Energy in motion. Emotions are feelings that exist in the past.

Empathy: A projection of personalities to another being so that a mutuality exists in the experience of understandings, feelings, and thoughts. One who is sensitive to the feelings and thoughts of another is an *empath*. Empaths often feel the physical sensations and emotions of another.

Empowerment: An individual's assertion of personal power, energy, force, and strength in all fields: spiritual, physical, mental, and magical.

Enabler: One who allows others to continue their unproductive patterns of behavior. See *Codependent* and *Drama Triangle*.

Endomorphic Energy: Energy that is emitted from the body into the aura and chakras. This energy comprises the defined space of where electromagnetic, psychic, astral, etheric, mental, emotional, and other auric vibrations exist in sentient beings.

Photos hold the endomorphic energy of the being that is in the photo.

Caught teachings emerge through Endomorphic energy. See *Aura* and *Chakras*.

Endoplasm: Endoplasm is the external psychic coverage of ectoplasm. The collective form of microcosms or unit consciousnesses with their coverage of endoplasm moves society as part of the collective consciousness. Such movement may well be referred to as the "collective psychology." Endoplasm also ensures that the ectoplasm maintains the psychic form necessary, so that the mind is not dissipated and mental propensities have an opportunity for expression in the cruder/material world. See *Consciousness*.

Energy Wave: Light sound and light energy move in waves. Healers ride these waves through crests and troughs, the high points and low points, because this is the way that energy moves to heal the healee. See *Crest* and *Troughs*.

Enlightenment: Being in a state of all-knowing, unqualified knowledge. This is the state of living outside of illusions and living in bliss. This state involves complete universal consciousness in which the mind is full of light.

Entities: Discarnates or spirit beings without physical bodies that can be seen or recognized by some, but undetectable by others. They continue to live between physical incarnations. They are often beings who, after death, do not cross over; instead they continue to exist in spirit form. Some visitation and contact between planes is noted; their presence may be positive or negative. See *Discarnate Being*.

Entity Removal: Exorcism. The process of separating a parasitic discarnate being from the field of the healee, and sending that being to the light.

Esoteric: Understood by or intended for a chosen few (for example, an inner group of disciples or initiates). Pertaining to something beyond the understanding or knowledge of the average person.

Essential Oils: Fluid extracted from botanical sources, preserved in pure form, and used in aromatherapy. They are usually blended and diluted with basic carrier oils; these oils can contain energies that can help shift and balance the aura. See *Aromatherapy* and *Aura*.

Etheric Energy: Our energetic soup. It is a personal mixture of emotions, intentions, and fears that exist in the first subtle body. Etheric energy is positive or negative energy emitted from a person's body, and mixes with the soup of the next person they encounter, which then mixes with the soup of the next and so on. See *Aura*.

Etheric Plane: The name of the plane upon which Etheric energy exists.

Ethics: The code or philosophy we develop and adopt that protects personal integrity and leads to peace of mind and establishes harmony between inner and outer. See *Integrity*.

Fear: The feeling that generally arises when love is not present. A feeling that occurs whenever we are in danger, when we feel threatened, or when we perceive danger. Fears can be founded on personal experiences, natural instincts, or embedded in us through the experience of others.

Feeler: A person who receives information from the kinesthetic sense; a kinesthetic learner.

Feeling: A NOW-time emotional experience.

Feng Shui: Ancient Chinese art of orienting objects, buildings, and towns to promote a healthy flow of chi. All areas, large and small, have a distinctive energy that can be enhanced by rearranging objects (for example, removing an ornament from an apartment or adding an object to a particular corner of a room). See *Chi*.

Filling: Filling the healee with healing energy. See *Closing, Primary Essence,* and *Secondary Essence*.

Fire Element: The Element of Fire is one of the quicker elements used in healing. The challenge with Fire is that once the energy is flowing, it may be difficult to get it to stop because Fire tends to consume all that is in its path. When Fire is being used, there is a tendency for both healer and healee to get hot. See *Air, Earth, Healing,* and *Water Elements*.

Fire Walking: An empowering ritual that involves mind over matter. Participants walk barefoot over hot coals without getting burned, thus expanding their concept of their capabilities and strengthening their connection to Source.

Flower Essences: A technique that uses extracts from flowering plants in homeopathic proportions as catalysts for healing. Each liquid preparation carries the energetic imprint of a specific plant, affecting the aura and working on the root causes of disease.

Foot Chakras: The chakras in the bottom of the feet that are used both to ground and to move healing energies from Source or from the Earth. See *Chakra* and *Grounding*.

Force (vs. strength): Energetic power flowing from Source.

Forgiveness: To set free of judgment, according to the book, *A Course in Miracles* (by Foundation for Inner Peace, 2007).

Four Directions: The spirits of North, South, East, West. These four spirits anchor the Universe that we know. They rule the seasons and days. The rising and setting of the sun gives us time and defines our days. The poles define our space. The seasons set the calendar and the year. We plant in the spring, in the summer our crops mature, we harvest in autumn, and in the winter the fields lay dormant, resting for the new life in the spring. Each direction offers a lesson for each phase of our lives. See *East, North, South,* and *West Directions*.

Four Elements: There are four basic Elements to work with during the healing process, and sometimes they are referred to as the *healing Elements*. These Elements are the driving catalysts for the transformation of matter. Each time there is a change on the physical plane, one of these elements is involved directly or in conjunction with the laws of physics. See *Air, Earth, Fire, Water,* and *Healing Elements*.

Free Will: Whether healing occurs or does not occur depends upon the conscious and subconscious/unconscious free will (choice) of the healee. Humans possess the ability to choose pleasure or pain, growth or stagnation, love or fear. Each choice, whether it appears to be negative or positive, serves the evolution or the devolution of the soul.

$\mathcal{G}$

God-Self: A person's inner voice; higher-self.

Gratitude: An attitude of thankfulness. Gratitude anchors in healing energy and magic.

Grounding: This is the process of staying with your feet on the ground (and, most importantly, with the chakras in the bottoms of the feet open) so that the energies can flow *in* the bottom of the left and *out* the bottom of the right. In a healing, grounding is the conscious connection to Earth that involves the process of staying in touch with the physical so that the energies of the healee's disease can move through the healer and into earth, which is closer to the healee's vibratory rate than Source is. The earth will then absorb used energies and transmute the energies from old to new. See *Centering* and *Foot Chakras.*

Guide: A member of an individual's spirit group who assumes the roles of protecting, guiding, and influencing daily life and destiny, and assists in creating an understanding of spiritual truths. See *Power Animal.*

Guided Imagery: An exercise to develop the imagination in which a guide leads people to visualize through suggestions and symbols.

H

Hand Chakras: The chakras that are centered in the palms of the hands. Usually, when employing hands-on healing techniques, the healing energy moves through the hand chakras of the healer into the healee. See *Chakra*.

Healee: The person or animal to which a healer directs the energies to from Source.

Healer: The person or thing serving as a conduit for healing energies from Source to a healee.

Healing Crisis: During the initial phase of healing, as the body begins to clean house (detoxify) and the vital energy begins to repair and rebuild internal organs, healees may experience headaches, uneasiness, flu-like symptoms, and fatigue. It is important that they rest during this time. These symptoms will pass as the body becomes accustomed to a new level of energy. *The healee may feel worse before he or she feels better.* The healee eventually reaches a plateau of better health. During the healing crisis, it is important not to suppress these temporary symptoms with drugs, which may interrupt the healing process.

Healing Field: The combined energies of all forces, all people present, and the energies of the physical plane, space, or building in the healing situation. The most important aspect of this field is the field of integrity. See *Integrity*.

Healing Space: The area in which the healing is happening. It includes the energy that is present from the building, the building's owner, and past events that have occurred in this space.

Heart Chakra: The fourth energy center located halfway between the three lower chakras and the three higher chakras. This chakra is the center of love, and acts as a bridge between the physical and spiritual. It is associated with the color green and the musical note F. See *Chakra, Seven Chakra System,* and *Twelve Chakra System.*

High Magic: The art of white magic where the practitioner knows what to do and expect, and no longer has to depend on rites or tools; instead he or she relies on psychic powers. The magician uses *thought to accomplish this.* High magic works with the Higher Planes of Spirit, and closer to Spirit. Practitioners need to be pretty evolved on their path to use it effectively. See *Black Magic, Low Magic, Magic, Middle Magic,* and *White Magic.*

Higher Self: The super-conscious or higher-conscious mind.

Hydration: Water conducts energy. Our bodies are made mostly of water. It is therefore important for the healer and healee to drink plenty of water before and after a healing. See *Dehydration* and *Water Element.*

/
=

I AM: Man's sacred connection to the God that dwells within, also a particular affirmation to invoke this Divine (Source: "all there is, was, and will be") consciousness.

I Ching: *Book of Changes,* a Chinese oracle and philosophical text based on a deep understanding of yin and yang; consisting of 64 hexagrams, each symbolizing archetypal energies or situations. Collected by the Duke of Chou, c. 1500; principal commentary by Confucius. See *Yin and Yang.*

Initiation: The transition from one point of polarization to another, which creates a growing capacity to see and hear on all planes and leads to an expansion of consciousness; a brief period of enlightenment wherein the initiate sees that portion of their path that lies ahead and shares consciously in the evolutional plan.

Integrity: The quality of consistently living out our commitments and walking our talk.

Intuition: Intuition opens up the world of ideas to us, thus providing correct ideas and a correct knowledge of reality. Although common usage denotes emotional impulses with a faint content of the lowest mental consciousness, in reality the term refers to consciousness at the causal level or higher. Most philosophers are still in the two lowest domains of deductive thinking and principle thinking. A few people have worked their way up through the different layers of mental consciousness to achieve the consciousness of intuition.

J

Judgments: It is essential for healers to drop any judgments and view the healee from a soul level in order to understand the Divine plan at work, no matter how "bad" the situation may seem.

K

Karma: From Hinduism and Buddhism, this is the sum and consequences of a person at any time and during all lifetimes. It is the recorded accounting for all good, evil, and indifference that follow the entity and determine the soul's destiny in future reincarnations. Karma is the natural law of cause and effect, and is constantly created.

Karmic Debt: The accumulation of negation in one's karma at any particular time that affects the life path.

Kinesiology: Muscle testing in which the person holds the substance in question while being tested for muscular resistance responses.

Kinesthetic: The modality through which a person senses energies through feelings, rather than the visual, auditory, olfactory, or gustatory. See *Feeler.*

$$L$$

Letting Go: The process of surrendering control to a higher power; a process of releasing old, used energy or patterns that no longer serve us.

Life Force: See *Prana.*

Light Language: Ancient Mayan system of healing and manifesting, using the energies of specific colors and sacred geometries in sequences called *grids.* These grids act as a very loud prayer and shift the aura of the person, group, object, or place to magnetize the desired outcome.

Light Senses: The five nonphysical senses that a healer employs for emanating or detecting energy. See *Charismatic, Electric, Electromagnetic, Magnetic,* and *Presence.*

Light Worker: Anyone who participates in increasing the light on Earth in order to raise its vibration. Positive thoughts, kind words and deeds, prayer, compassion, and many other things increase the light on the planet.

Low Magic: A form of magic that uses *tools*—physical plane items/objects (sword, branches, cards, crystals, candles, runes). Low magic is not "lower," it is simply closer to the physical plane. See *Black Magic, High Magic, Magic, Middle Magic,* and *White Magic.*

Lymphatic System: The lymphatic system is a system of vessels that assists the veins in recovering the body's tissue fluids and returning them to the heart. The lymphatic system cleans and clears the body, the aura, the subtle bodies, and the chakras all at once. It forms a braid of three rainbows that extends throughout our bodies. When we are missing a color from one of these braids, we begin to form a disease. When we are missing a color from two braids, the disease becomes matter. When we are missing a color from three braids, the disease becomes chronic.

$$\mathcal{M}$$

Magic: The practice of manipulating and controlling the course of nature by preternatural means. Magic is based upon the belief that the Universe is populated by unseen forces or spirits that permeate all things. Because human beings seek to control nature, and because these supernatural forces are thought to govern the course of natural events, the control of these forces gives humans control over nature. The practice of magic is held to depend upon the proper use of both the ritual and the spell. The spell, or incantation, is the core of the magical ceremony; it unlocks the full power of the ritual. The practice of magic, in seeking its desired end, also frequently combines within its scope elements of religion and science. See *Black Magic, High Magic, Low Magic, Middle Magic,* and *White Magic.*

Magnetic: One of the five light senses. This is the light sense that pulls the healers' hands toward the spots on the healee. See *Charismatic, Electric, Electromagnetic,* and *Presence.*

Mandala: An intricate pattern of concentric circles, squares, polygons, and other geometric or artistic symbols representing the Order of the Universe, and used for instruction or meditation.

Manifestation: We each create our own reality through the manifestation of outcomes based on our thoughts and feelings. Every single thing in life, whether it be a material object, an event, or an experience, began as a thought. Our thoughts create everything around us. If we wish to change our lives, we first begin with changing our thoughts in order to create our lives the way we want them to be. Manifestation makes each of us responsible for our lives.

Mantra: A meditative tool involving the use of a sacred sound consisting of words or syllables (meaningful or meaningless) whose sounds produce psychic or spiritual effects.

Material World: Everything that is connected to a person materially (for example, your cash, your home, your car, and so on).

Medicine Wheel: An ancient stone circle that has been used for thousands of years by Native people as a place for prayer, ceremony, and self-understanding. The stones are set up to symbolize various aspects of the Universe.

Meditation: Meditation can be any process or technique we use to alter our brain waves and set aside our conscious mind in order to get in touch with the Divine within.

Medium: A person who, in a state of trance, is able to allow discarnate spirits to enter the emotional world. Genuine esoteric teachers (members of the planetary hierarchy) do not use mediums to contact people. And quite the opposite, they warn against using mediums, which conflicts with the law of self-realization; it also harms the medium physically and "morally." See *Clairvoyance.*

Mental Plane: The plane upon which our thought processes and thought forms exist and are created.

Meridian: Streams of energy that flow through the physical body to keep *chi*, or life force, distributed to all systems, organs, and cells. If imbalanced or out of harmony, the flow is affected. See *Acupuncture* and *Chi.*

Metaphysics: Metaphysics is the study of that which is not physical, and that which cannot be perceived using the five physical or heavy senses of touch, taste, hearing, vision and smell. Meta means "above" or "beyond," and therefore *metaphysical* means "beyond our physical world." Our "metaphysical senses" include clairvoyance, clairaudience, clairsentience, telepathy, and telekinesis. The word *metaphysics* can also include the full range of studies from mystical philosophies through occultism, positive thinking, legends, myths, allegorical writings, comparative ancient or contemporary religions, and the world of strange and unusual phenomena, such as Bigfoot, ghosts, and UFOs. The classical meaning of *metaphysics* is "physics above the physical." Today, most people believe that if they hold positive attitudes, and believe in guides or guardian angels, space brothers, UFOs, interdimensional beings, or channeling, they are into the field of metaphysics; however unless they grasp the full meaning of their real nature in a living universe, they have barely begun to understand the higher physics. See *Clairvoyance, Clairaudience, Clairsentience*.

Middle Magic: The magician gets in the middle of two entities (person/thing). This is not typically used in basic healings. Middle magic is used for stopping things such as curses, hexes, and spells. See *Black Magic, High Magic, Low Magic, Magic,* and *White Magic*.

Miracle: A Divine intervention in the mind, which heals thought patterns and assists the individual in making a quantum leap or achieving extraordinary results not previously thought possible.

Mudras: Various hand gestures symbolizing different meanings that can shift and redirect the energy of a person or group. Mudras are effectively used in meditation, healing, and public speaking.

NLP (Neuro-Linguistic Programming): A psychology of communications that focuses on the link between linguistics and physical factors including tone of voice, pitch, body posture, and eye movements. Understanding and working with this system can help one build rapport with coworkers, healees, and students. See *Auditory Modality* and *Visionary Modality.*

North Direction: One of the Four Directions. A place of wisdom. People with an affinity to the North are very grounded and lean toward stability. Associated with Earth. See *East, Four Directions, West,* and *South.*

Numerology: Every number has its own vibration, and numerology is the study of these vibrations and how they affect people. The numeric vibrations of a person's name, birthplace, and birth date can give information about his or her personality, capabilities, and future.

Old Soul: One who has reincarnated many times.

Om: (Pronounced *Aum*). A mantra believed to be the manifest symbol of the cosmic energy or God. It is a sacred Sanskrit syllable symbolizing the sum total of all energy. It represents first cause, omnipresent sound, and lasting peace.

Paradigm: A set of deep concepts about the nature of reality that shapes language, thought, perceptions, and system structures.

Paradigm Shift: Spiritual or mental axis shift; a change in perception or world view, such as the Copernican, Darwinian, Freudian, or New Age revolution.

Past Healing: Healing something from one's past.

Patterns: Crystallized energetic imprints that repeat throughout one's life, causing various types of dis-ease. In order to heal a pattern, acknowledgment from the person is required.

Pendulum: A divinatory tool often used to communicate with spirits or the divine. See *Low Magic.*

Permission: Before a healing, the healee must first ask clearly for the healing. Sometimes the healee will request advice and come back again and again for more advice on the same situation, yet they will have not put that advice into action in their lives. This continual request for advice is a form of asking for healing. However, when people *complain* about something, they are not *asking* for a healing. They must ask the healer *how to change* it before the healer can work on them.

Persecutor: One of three players in the drama triangle. The persecutor is extremely critical and rigid, and leads by using threats and giving orders. This person often feels inadequate underneath the bully façade. See *Codependent, Drama Triangle, Rescuer,* and *Victim.*

Personality: The aspect of our individual consciousness that is expressed in human form.

Physical Plane: The densest plane of existence where energy is converted into matter, and matter becomes form.

Pineal Gland: A small gland located between the cerebral hemispheres of the brain that secretes melatonin.

Pingala: (Sanskrit) Subtle nerve channel on the right side of the spine; channel used for directing kundalini energy and chakra work.

Polarities: See *Yin and Yang.*

Power Animal: An animal spirit that acts as a person's guide and protector. See *Guide.*

Power Up: A method of working with energy in such a way as to raise the vibration of a person, group, or place.

Prana: Prana is the vital life force that flows through the channels of our bodies. Many believe that prana can be breathed into the body from the heavens, and that it is the element that keeps us alive. Without prana, one's physical body cannot exist. While most people think that it is air (oxygen) that keeps our bodies alive, metaphysical people believe that it is the prana that we breathe in along *with* the oxygen that keeps us alive.

Prayer: To stand in the presence of God and let Him/Her fill your heart with love, light, and power.

Presence: One of the five light senses. This is the light sense that, when strongly developed, can heal and affect others who are present in this being's energy field. The type of energy from Source that comes through presence is one that gives a feeling of all-around well-being. Presence is a wide, soft, feel-good beam. See *Charismatic, Electric, Magnetic,* and *Electromagnetic.*

Primary Essence: Primary qualities such as bliss, wisdom, trust, wealth, truth, light, peace, value, and so on. Used for closing a healee at the end of the session. Healers should choose carefully when closing someone with an essence. The essence has to be in line with their path and is not necessarily what they want; it is what they need. See *Closing, Filling,* and *Secondary Essence.*

Processing: The systematic steps of letting go of used energies, becoming clear, and resetting our energies at the next level.

Projection: The act of putting our "stuff" onto another person, or blaming, rather than taking ownership and responsibility.

Psychokinesis: A technique of mind over matter through invisible means that can result in the movements of objects, bending of metals, and determining the outcome of events. It can occur spontaneously and deliberately, which indicates it is both an unconscious and conscious process.

Quantum Physics: Quantum physics was developed mostly in the 20th century; it deals with microscopic properties—the charge, mass, spin, and so on, of elementary particles. Quantum physics is unique in that it takes into consideration the mind of the scientist or the observer of physical matter, who may have an effect on what is being observed. Therefore, the idea of traditional science as being objective is questionable, and the laws of pure material physics may not be as useful to science, for the mind of the observer may be affecting the scientific experiments.

R

Rage Work: Techniques used to help people heal repressed anger. One method involves beating a pillow with a plastic bat while verbalizing the rage. See *Angry*.

Reality: Actuality is what actually is, while reality is based on individual perception of actuality.

Rebirthing: A process that involves deep-breathing techniques and a reenactment of the birth process in order to heal repressed attitudes and emotions. A human continues to be reborn as a human until he or she has mastered all of the qualities and abilities necessary to enable him or her to continue his or her conscious expansion.

Reflexology: A healing system based on the manipulation of reflex points on the feet or hands. These points correspond to specific organs, and places on and within the body.

Reiki: A Japanese healing technique that taps into the Universal Life Energy, which can heal and balance all living beings.

Remote Healing: See *Absent Healing*.

Rescuer: One of the three players in the drama triangle. They focus on helping others to avoid their own problems. They are usually angry underneath and tend to be lonely because they do not have a life of their own. They help (meddle) without being asked to do so. They often play the role of martyr. See *Codependent, Drama Triangle, Persecutor,* and *Victim.*

Residue: The excess or leftover energies resulting from the letting go of energies in a healing. When the healer clears the field, a part of the process is removing some of the residual energies, while leaving others that may be removed at a later time.

Resistance: Not going with the flow. "What you resist persists."

Resonance: All of the energies, as they combine, form the field for healing. This is resonate to a vibratory rate that is a combination of all forces at play and the innate energies that apply to the healing. The overall quality of the healing depends on the awareness of the healer to the energies present and his or her ability to use them for the highest good of all concerned.

Ritual: A prayerful act performed with intention in order to anchor in a specific energy. The more often a ritual is performed, the greater its power.

Root Chakra: First energy center located at the base of the spine and also referred to as the *base chakra.* Associated with survival and life force. Its color is red and it is associated with the musical note C. See *Chakra, Seven Chakra System,* and *Twelve Chakra System.*

Rounding: Rounding is the method of taking the edges off the field as the healing progresses. As more and more used energies are driven out of the bodies of the healee, they tend to collect at the edges of the field, especially when they are moving rapidly.

Runes: A tool of magic and divination. There are many types of runes including Anglo-Saxon, Wiccan, and Norse. They all represent a type of alphabet. After deciding a subject, the runes are usually tossed randomly and then deciphered based on their positioning.

S

Sacral Chakra: Second energy center located in the abdominal region. Associated with creation and cocreation (and sex). Also called the sexual chakra. It is orange in color and associated with the musical note D. See *Chakra, Seven Chakra System,* and *Twelve Chakra System.*

Sacred Geometry: This is the study of the underlying invisible geometric structure of all matter. Everything in existence has an underlying invisible geometric structure that makes a shape and forms what it is in the natural world.

Sacred Space: Esperanza, Starr Fuentes' Curandera teacher, taught that "Sacred Space is proportional to the exact amount of clean, clear floor space, times the width that a healer can hold." What makes a space sacred to us is often bound up with our sense of identity. By knowing that "miracles happen here," we have a sense of touching time beyond ourselves, and in doing so, we evolve and awaken to a larger paradigm. Sacred Space involves knowing where we are, who we are, who we have been, and who we might become. We know Source by many names—Jesus, Buddha, and so on; however, it is the original place where we grasped a deeper meaning of Source and increased our level of participation that opens up to the place of the spiritual rite of passage. Sacred Space is where we experience Source as concrete in the form of manifestations. It is a place where we come face to face with our own spiritual power. Sacred Space provides a safe place for us to focus on the spiritual.

Sad: Affected with or expressive of grief or unhappiness; of little worth.

Scared: Filled with fear or apprehension, filled with concern or regret over an unwanted situation, or having a dislike for something. See *fear*.

Science: The systematic study of how the physical and material plane energies work, using instruments. Many recent scientific discoveries that have been made about healing and quantum physics have been known to the Shamans and the masters for thousands of years.

Secondary Essence: Secondary qualities that end in *y, ing, ion,* and *ly.* To fill someone with understanding limits him or her. Fill them with wisdom, a primary essence, instead. See *Closing, Filling,* and *Primary Essence.*

Service: Approaching life from an attitude of service is the easiest, safest, quickest path to evolution. Although service is not about receiving, when a person *unconditionally* does a service of any kind, he or she will automatically burn karma and reap many rewards. Those who serve mankind unselfishly receive more and more opportunities to serve.

Seven Chakra System: Traditional metaphysical science teaches that there are seven primary chakras associated with the body. Starting at the top of the head, these chakras are generally referred to as the crown chakra, brow (third eye) chakra, throat chakra, heart chakra, solar plexus chakra, sexual (sacral) chakra, and base (root) chakra. However, a significant aspect of the mutational changes, involves the activation of additional chakras. See *Chakra* and *Twelve Chakra System.*

Shaman: A medicine man/woman or witch doctor.

Shamanism: The religion of the ancient peoples of northern Europe and Asia, generally characterized by the ability of the Shaman to communicate with the spirit world. Major facets of Shamanism are animism, possession, prophecy/revelations, shapeshifting, and soul travel.

Silver Cord: The cord of consciousness invisible in physical reality, which allows us to leave the physical body, yet remain connected to it while engaging in astral travel or projection. This cord looks like an umbilical cord and is attached at the solar plexus, heart, or top of head. When we die, it is severed so that we can cross over to the other side.

Solar Plexus Chakra: Third energy center located in the stomach region. Associated with power, intuition, and clarity. Its color is yellow and is associated with the musical note E. See *Chakra, Seven Chakra System,* and *Twelve Chakra System.*

Soul: Immortal essence of all beings.

South Direction: One of the four directions. It stands for the peak of life, warmth, understanding, and ability. People with affinity to this direction embody certain characteristics, such as innocence, faith, and trust. See *East, Four, North,* and *West Directions.*

Spirit Guides: Spirit guides are the physical and nonphysical entities who have chosen to aid others on the path to spiritual enlightenment. These beings of light may physically appear in humanoid form, so that the mind can conceptualize them. Most spirit guides have incarnated on the physical Earth plane, as well as in other realms. See *Guide* and *Power Animal.*

Spiritual plane: The plane of existence in which our spiritual energies reside or express themselves.

Subconscious: Humans are constantly receiving impulses from the subconscious mind. Each incarnation leaves its own layer of consciousness within the subconscious mind. All of this is preserved as rudiments of qualities and abilities, usually manifesting as potential. It is important to develop the rudimentary potentials in each new incarnation, a process which becomes increasingly easier each time, in order for them to be actualized.

Subtle Bodies: The layers of the auric field that contain valuable information about the health and well-being of the individual.

$$T$$

Talisman: A magically charged object used to attract a certain type of energy or a particular type of person. See *Low Magic.*

Tarot: A form of divination using a set of cards (usually 76 cards) that represent human archetypes. See *Low Magic.*

Taught Teaching: Information that is formally taught (spoken or written) by a teacher to a student and received by the conscious mind. See *Caught Teaching.*

Techniques: The purpose of techniques in a healing is to control the way and type of energy that flows into the healee. Techniques fine-tune, smooth, and alter the energy, so that the different parts of the body receive energy in forms that are appropriate to raise the level of vitality.

Theta Wave: Brain wave associated with meditation, memory, learning enhancement, and vivid imagery. See *Alpha Wave* and *Beta Wave.*

Third Eye Chakra: Also known as the *sixth chakra,* or the *brow chakra,* this chakra is located approximately 1 inch above the eyebrows, and centered between them. The third eye chakra deals with our wisdom, spirituality, and psychic awareness. Its color is purple or indigo. It is associated with the musical note A. See *Chakra, Seven Chakra System,* and *Twelve Chakra System.*

Thought Forms: When a person thinks, a portion of their mental envelope is ejected into the surrounding mental world where it immediately assumes a form that is determined by the content and quality of the thought. See *Manifestation.*

Throat Chakra: Fifth energy center located in the throat and associated with communication. Its color is blue and it is associated with the musical note G. See *Chakra, Seven Chakra System,* and *Twelve Chakra System.*

Totem: Nonhuman entity, often represented as an animal, that symbolizes the spiritual essence, and often the first ancestor of a group.

Transformation: A rebirthing of self while in the same physical form, which involves the systematic processes of letting go of deeply ingrained patterns, thereby creating a space for significant evolution.

Transmission: The delivery of caught teachings from a master teacher to a student. See *Caught Teachings.*

Transmutation: The alchemical conversion of one energy into another. In the healing process, unhealthy patterns are transformed into new healthy patterns.

Trough: Part of the healing wave when the energy from Source seems to diminish. All the body's systems and energy systems are integrating the energy. At this point in time, it is important for the healer to let the integration process happen; this is not the time to push the energies or to open up wider to Source. This is a great point to clean out the energy of the field because at this time, Source is moving out the used energy. See *Crest* and *Energy Wave.*

Trust: Trust equals "true us." The clear recognition of what you or another person will be or do, and won't be or do. Trust is knowledge that is based on past experiences with someone, which leads us to be confident (or not) in the capabilities or the intentions in another person or self. In healings, it is essential for the healer to trust all the processes at work during the healing session.

Twelve Chakra System: The activation of additional chakras is a significant aspect of the mutational changes many Light Workers are undergoing at this time. Many of us are moving into the twelve chakra system. In the book *Bringers of the Dawn* by Barbara J. Marciniak (Bear & Company, 1992), the Pleiadians indicate that five additional chakras, which are located outside of the body, are in the process of being activated. In this frame of reference, the eighth chakra is located slightly above the head. Chakras nine through 12 are considered to be located well above the head. These are approximate locations; these extended chakras essentially transcend our space-time continuum, and thus the actual location is not significant. See *Chakra* and *Seven Chakra System*.

U

Unconscious: According to esoterics, the unconscious is a combination of subconsciousness and superconsciousness. The subconscious is the latent memory of past experiences, while the superconscious consists of a long series of domains of consciousness as yet not conquered.

V

Vedic Medicine: See *Auryruveda*.

Victim: Player in the drama triangle characterized by "poor me" thinking. The victim feels victimized, oppressed, helpless, hopeless, powerless, and ashamed. The victim looks for a rescuer who will perpetuate these negative feelings. As long as this person stays in the victim position, he or she blocks himself or herself from making decisions, solving problems, enjoying pleasure, and understanding the self. See *Codependent, Drama Triangle, Persecutor*, and *Rescuer*.

Vision Quest: Native American spiritual search characterized by solitude, fasting, and dreams.

Visionary Modality: NLP (Neuro-linguistic Programming) learning style that involves the sense of sight as the primary means of perception. See *NLP.*

Vortex: The funnel shape created by a whirling fluid or by the motion of spiraling energy. Familiar examples of vortex shapes are whirlwinds, tornadoes, and water going down a drain. A vortex can be made up of anything that flows, such as wind, water, or electricity. Energy vortexes are swirling centers of subtle energy coming out from the surface of the Earth. The vortex energy is not exactly electrical or magnetic, although it does leave a slight measurable residual magnetism in the places where it is strongest.

Water Element: Water is a flowing Element. During a healing, Water tends to flow in to cleanse and fill all the areas where it can find access. Water can carry most of the light energy by its ability to conduct energy. It is recommended to use small quantities of Water energy as it is easier to control and use in a vitalizing manner. Side effects from working with this energy include a runny nose, crying, excessive urinating, or vomiting. See *Air, Earth, Fire,* and *Healing Elements.*

West Direction: One of the four directions. It is the place where the rain originates, and also a place that represents the end, or finality, as things done in the dark are final things. People with an affinity for the West may become *heyoka,* meaning "sacred clown," which does everything backward or in a contrary manner. The bald eagle is associated with this direction. See *East, Four, North,* and *South Directions.*

White Magic: Magic that is *for* or *in favor of* something. If you are *for* your goal, it is *white* magic. For example, being *for* sobriety is *white* magic; being *against* drunk driving is *black* magic. Think of *for* energy as open, flowing, and seeking the positive. Inevitably, white magic will accomplish more. See *Black Magic, High Magic, Low Magic, Middle Magic,* and *Magic.*

$$\mathcal{Y}$$

Yin and Yang: Fundamental principles of Chinese philosophy. Yin corresponds to energy that is negative, dark, passive, cold, wet, and feminine. Yang corresponds to energy that is positive, bright, active, dry, hot, and masculine. In people and in nature, the interactions and balance of yang energy with its yin counterpart influences health and behavior.

Index

Index

* * * * * * * * * * * * * * * *

* * * * * * * * * * * * * *

About the Author

Starr Fuentes has accumulated vast knowledge of esoteric information from five decades of study with masters around the world, a lifetime of using healing techniques, and from teaching thousands of students.

Her life and healing path

Starr was born in 1939 in the slums of Detroit, the daughter of a Polish mother and Mexican father. Alcoholism ravaged her parents' lives, and Starr spent her childhood hungry, cold, and abused, the victim of physical neglect and sexual violence. Starr's only sister committed suicide at the age of 13, when Starr was only six years old.

As a child, Starr had comfort in only two places—the library and with her grandmother. Starr would stay in the warmth and comfort of the library, reading every night until the library closed. She explored all the exotic and foreign lands that she would one day visit, and fed her voracious hunger for knowledge. Starr's genius-level intelligence went completely unnoticed by her parents, but through the help of a young friend and his family, Starr joined Mensa at age 11.

Psychic abilities were as common as alcoholism in her family, and Starr became aware of her special gifts at a young age. Her grandmother was a practicing healer, and Starr spent endless hours in her kitchen, learning the art of herbs, healing, and magic. Even from the crib, Starr recalls seeing auras. In school, when she'd make drawings of people and animals, she'd draw in the aura quite naturally, not initially understanding that this was unusual. She began to recognize illness in others through the colors of their auras. She quickly learned that people were afraid of her abilities, and for many years considered her gifts "a cruel joke."

When she was 13, Starr left home and began supporting herself by becoming a waitress at a truck stop. She went to college on a full scholarship, waiting on tables at night and teaching yoga. Starr finally came to terms with her healing abilities during her senior year in college, after she put her hand over the tumor of a friend and it manifested into her palm. She knew she had a few choices—drown herself in alcohol like her parents, or step into who she was being called to be. She chose to become a healer.

Starr's healing path

Starr stepped onto the healer's path consciously and began to use her psychic abilities in many ways, doing readings for people and assisting local and federal agencies in solving crimes.

Starr made her first journey to study with a master in Colombia. From there, she went to Mexico City, then on to study with

the Mexican Curanderos in Vera Cruz, where she spent three years with her main teacher, Esperanza. Starr traveled the world, studying with shamans in South America and Mexico, barefoot doctors in China, lamas in India, and witch doctors in Africa. She studied Tantric sex in India to rid herself of her sexual traumas, becoming a master in her own right.

During her three years with Esperanza, Starr worked very hard. Long hours were spent healing the hundreds of people who came from miles around. Makeshift healing tables were set up and meals were eaten in haste and short breaks allowed for little else other than the basics. At the end of the day, Starr was too exhausted to care about sleeping in a hammock strung up outdoors. Starr's apprenticeship taught her many things, including sacred service, honoring her master teacher, and preserving the integrity of the lineage. Her appreciation and gratitude grew beyond measure.

After many years of studying various healing techniques all over the world, Starr returned to the Western hemisphere to teach others to mend their own wounds and eventually to heal cancer. Starr has brought thousands of men, women, and children to emotional, mental, and physical health with her eclectic use of ancient healing techniques, modern psychological tools, her psychic abilities, deep compassion for human suffering, and her sense of humor. She has the ability to see a person's essence and calls us to our highest levels of possibility.

Starr currently operates a retreat center in Texas as well as the Divine Intervention Dome conference/spiritual center in Hot Springs, Arizona. In addition to teaching at the Dome, she travels monthly to teach from her more than 400 classes, of which the most popular are: Light Language, Divine Intervention, Soul Pulling, 12 Strand DNA, and Dimensional Mastery. Starr has several meditations and information podcasts available on iTunes, as well as many Websites, including *www.starrfuentes.com* and *www.didome.com*.

* * * * * * * * * * * * * * *

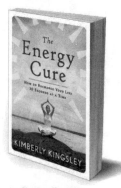